Ferrari's World Champions

The cars that beat the world

INTRODUCTION
BY PINO ALLIEVI

GIORGIO NADA EDITORE

Ferrari's World

Champions

i n d e x

Ferrari's World

Champions

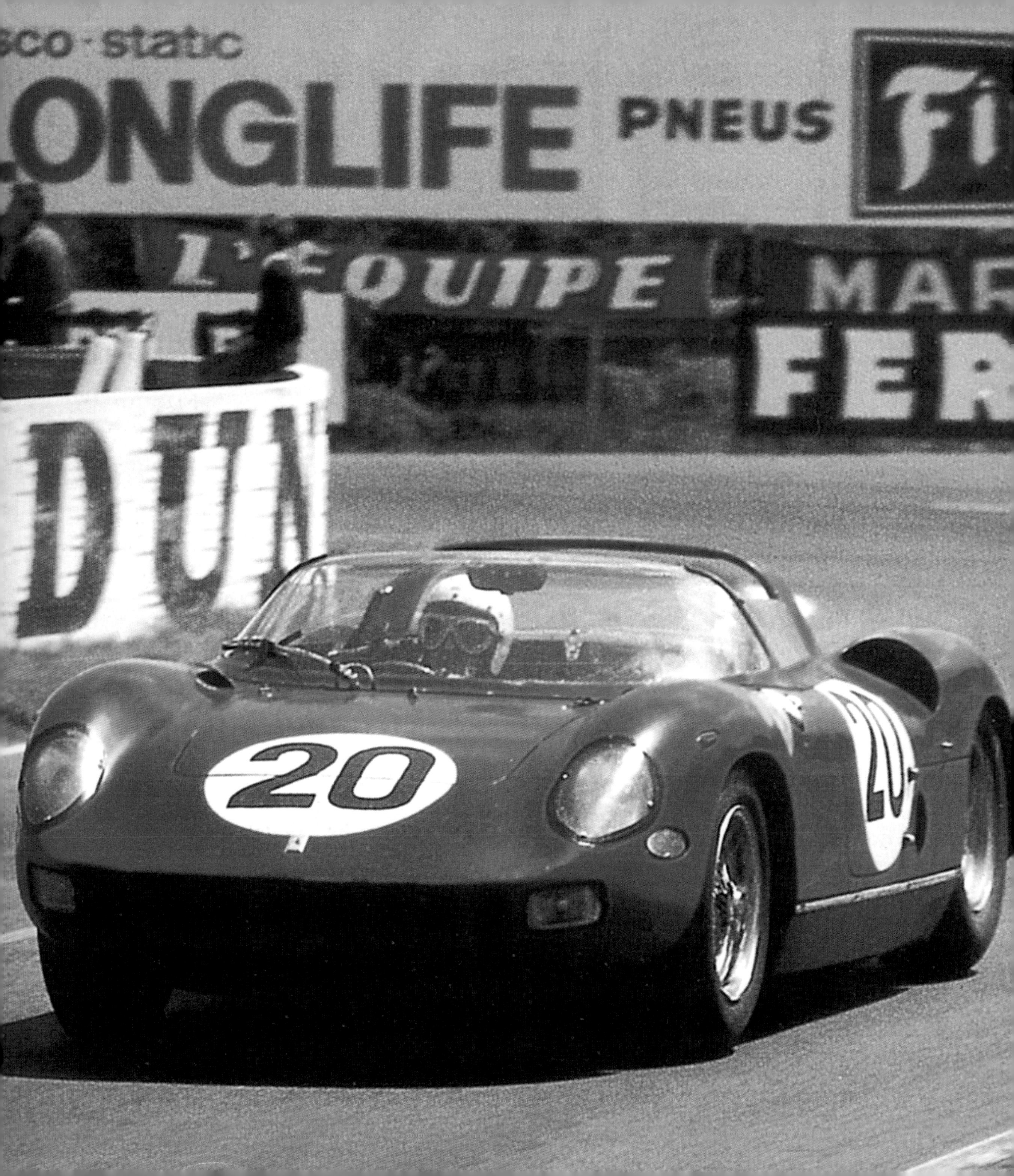

sco · static
LONGLIFE
PNEUS
L'EQUIPE
MAR
FER
DUN
20

A winter afternoon, around 2 pm. My home 'phone rings, Franco Gozzi with his priestly voice hands me over to Enzo Ferrari, who is furious. He is annoyed with the British constructors, who want to defend mini-skirts at all costs. "Why don't you come over here and I'll tell you a few interesting things," he asks. So I leave home. In a couple of hours I arrive at Maranello. The factory traffic light, the road to the right for Motor Sport Management. The bar is raised, the office is right after the entrance. Gozzi, who covers the jobs of press officer, confidante, advisor, assistant, historic memory, archivist, master of ceremonies and entertainer, prepares what the "Boss" (that's what he called him) should tell me with a precise abundance of the details. And underlines that, if I want, I can also write something afterwards, without identifying my source.

"Ah, you've arrived. Yes, come in, come in", said Enzo Ferraro in a high-pitched voice from his office. The chair in black leather with its frame in steel is comfortable; the command centre of Ferrari is big. Behind him is a picture of Arturo Merzario with the prototype 312 P at the Targa Florio. The azure Venetian

Ferrari

blinds allow a small amount of light to filter in, outside it is pearl grey as if it is getting ready to snow. Fortunately, a lamp by a famous stylist on his desk has been switched on.

"So, what's happening in Milan? And at your newspaper? Did you hear about so-and-so…" He starts like that, with a long chat in which Ferrari talks to me about mini-skirts, which should be abolished for reasons of safety. And then he slips into many other topics, even talking about where he went on his honeymoon. Gozzi comes and goes, the secretary only switches through the telephone calls he has to take. Including one from a Milanese businessman who would later become the head of government, with whom Ferrari argues bitterly because the man on the other end was supposed to have said to a newspaper that "the Grand Old Man should step aside at his age".

But Enzo Ferrari is in excellent form; his age is just a number. When talking about his life, I ask him why he hasn't kept at least the cars that won his world championships as a kind of memento. With his right hand, he makes a gesture of irritation. "With the last, I could have actually done that, but I had to sell the first ones to help finance the factory. Every car becomes outdated as soon as it wins. The nice thing about racing cars is that they are never the same from one race to another: they fade right away, like beautiful women". Then he explains how he remembers with pleasure the 500 F2 that won the Ascari world titles, together with Lauda's 312 and Scheckter's T4. He recalls the effort put into building the necessary number of 512s for homologation, has an excellent recollection of the 312 Prototype created by a team of young engineers chosen by him. News. In reality, Ferrari does not intend

Opposite: Peter Collins in 1958 and (here, right) Kimi Raikkonen in 2008. In the history of Ferrari, Formula 1 Grands Prix have been a constant commitment, becoming a priority in the mid-Seventies. From then on, the Italian constructor's sporting future has been inexorably linked to the results achieved from races run on the tracks of the world. At the same time, the greater involvement of television has contributed to widening the audience of motor racing enthusiasts even further and, consequently, to the tifosi of the Rosse. Centre, left, the famous logo that has contributed to making Ferrari unique in the world and, more than anything else, the emblem of Enzo Ferrari who, after having received Prancing Horse as a gift from the family of the great fighter pilot Francesco Baracca, was already using it in the Thirties; at the time, when he was motor sport director of Alfa Romeo, he had it affixed to the Milanese racing cars.

Centre, right, a young Clay Regazzoni. Enzo Ferrari, who was also a racing driver in his youth, always had a special relationship with many of his drivers. For 30 years, great champions and excellent drivers have alternated in the Rosse and contributed with their remarkable exploits to building the Ferrari legend. Yet to the Commendatore, the merits of a victory could never be equally divided between man and car. In his extremely personal analysis of the equation, he always came out in favour of the car built at Maranello. Below, the 312 PB of 1972 being driven by Mario Andretti. Great results came from endurance racing which, until the mid-Seventies, were fundamental to the survival of Ferrari. Daytona and Le Mans were just two chapters, often triumphant, in a story which, in more than two decades, enabled Ferrari to win world titles and glory, but which also saw the company involved in great tragedies.

to look back but to look ahead. In fact he mentions, without giving too much away, Formula 1 for the next season, which will take place in a few weeks and for which feels curiosity, mixed with ill-concerned enthusiasm. Then, though, emerges his affection for various victories, certain cars, certain men who have driven them. The picture is completed in a vision of cause and effect, of experience that he adds to others, of lap times that continually get faster. And him at the centre, pretending that everything happened automatically, suggesting that the past is the past, like the pages of a riveting book that turn over to face the announced enthusiasm of those to come. Ferrari, obviously, knows it is not like that: his is just a huge excuse to distance nostalgia and the oppressive sense of time that is slipping away.

Pino Allievi

Formula 1

What is a race? How does one live it?

"It is a clamorous episode that today is concluded in Formula 1 in two hours of fascinating spectacle.
You must not forget endurance races,
like the 24 Hours of Le Mans,
Daytona or Sebring, where representation
mixes with a thousand unforeseen
human and technical adventures."

Enzo Ferrari

Ferrari

1952 - 500 F2
Single seater of champions

New regulations came in for the third season of the world championship which, in the final analysis, favoured Ferrari. Maranello already had an F2 single seater with a 4-cylinder, 2000 cc engine. In the two years that the title was competed for under those rules, the company humbled the competition by winning all the races valid for the world championship which it participate, except the last at Monza in 1953, which was won by Maserati, the Prancing Horse's historic rival in that period, with Argentinean Juan Manuel Fangio.

The constructional simplicity of both the chassis and engine was among the main advantages that enabled that car to snatch the world titles away from the potent Alfa Romeo 158 and 159, which had dominated the two previous seasons. The Ferraris were designed by Aurelio Lampredi, the creator of brilliant work, following the directives "ordered" by Enzo Ferrari: to design the first 4-cylinder in the history of the still young Modena company.

The drivers who raced the 500 F2 were also highly respected, starting with the man who won the two world championships. Alberto Ascari. The Milanese driver, who had battled for the world title until the last in the Grand Prix of Spain of the previous year, competed in 28 races with this car, winning 20 of them, and was still the protagonist even when he did not win. But this supremacy ended up reducing interest in those Grands Prix, with the tifosi already knowing how they would finish.

Next to the Milanese champion in the team there were also drivers of the calibre of Piero Taruffi, young Englishman Mike Hawthorn and ex-world champion Nino Farina, Ascari's close friend Gigi Villoresi, together with other less well known names who, however, enabled Maranello to write the first victorious chapter of a unique story that has continued for over 60 years.

The seasonal debut of Alberto Ascari on the track took place on 16 March 1952 with victory in the Grand Prix of Syracuse, which was not a world championship qualifier. Above, Ascari driving millimetres away from a trackside wall that lined a number of corners on the Sicilian circuit, where a year later the Milanese champion was forced into a double retirement, having also climbed into Mike Hawthorn's car on that occasion; the same one he drove to victory in 1952.
Below, a cutaway drawing of the 4-cylinder in-line 1,985 cc. This engine, designed by Aurelio Lampredi, generated a power output of 165 hp at 7,000 rpm; limits which, after various developments during the 1952 and 1953 seasons, was increased to almost 190 hp.

Above, left: Alberto Ascari in the pits at the Aerautodromo of Modena as he speaks to the celebrated journalist Giovanni Canestrini. The writer was one of the originators of the Mille Miglia, the event in which Alberto Ascari made his racing debut. It was 28 April 1940 and the race was run over a closed road route to be repeated three times on the Brescia-Cremona-Mantua triangle.

On that occasion, the Milanese champion was at the wheel of an 815 Auto Avio Costruzione roadster, the first car built by Enzo Ferrari which, however, could not carry his name due to agreements reached with Alfa Romeo. Ascari also competed in the post war Mille Miglia, retiring twice and scoring a splendid victory at the wheel of a Lancia D 24 in 1954.

Above, right: Alberto Ascari next to Enzo Ferrari. Relations between them were better than good, in part because of the respect that the Maranello constructor for the son of his great friend. Antonio Ascari, a champion many years earlier, was Ferrari's travelling companion in his motor sport adventure. Only at the end of 1953, following Alberto's move to Lancia was there a slightly frosty relationship

between the two. But this did not stop Ferrari from providing his ex-driver with a works single seater for the Grand Prix of Italy in September of the following year. After all, even Ferrari recognised Alberto's tremendous gifts: once the Milanese driver took the lead in a race, he was practically uncatchable, as the picture below, taken during his win at Syracuse in 1952, seems to confirm.

1953 | 500 F2

Enzo Ferrari chose talented drivers relying on their experience. In the two years of Ascari's unrivalled domination, other Ferrari drivers were still able to win world championship races in a 500 F2. One was Piero Taruffi in 1952 at Bern, where the man from Rome beat the opposition. The following year, young Mike Hawthorn and Nino Farina were victorious in the Grand Prix of Germany at the Nürburgring and the French GP at Reims respectively.

A number of static pictures of the glorious 500 F2 kept at the Museo dell'Automobile Carlo Biscaretti di Ruffia in Turin. The 500 F2 was the first Ferrari to dominate world motor racing. It was given its debut on 23 September 1951 at Modena and won, a prelude to a career that would bring to world titles to Maranello. The cars story is closely linked to the regulations imposed at the time by the Federation, which decided the 1952 and 1953 world championship seasons would be run under 52 rules in which the 500 F2 made its debut; only later was its cubic capacity increased to 2,500 and forced Ferrari to design the new 553 model for the 1954 world championship.

Below: the front row of the grid made up of four Ferraris at the Grand Prix of the City of Buenos Aires on 1 February 1953. Ascari, who had won on the same circuit with the 'usual' 500 F2 two weeks earlier, preferred to use the 375 with the 12-cylinder engine, introduced a few seasons earlier, but he retired. Victory went to his team mate Nino Farina, with Gigi Villoresi second. Both are shown next to Ascari's car number 18, the nose of which protrudes in the foreground.

In those two world championship years, Ferrari only employed Italian drivers Ascari, Farina, Taruffi, Villoresi, Maglioli and Carini. He made an exception with Frenchman André Simon for two 1952 races and the emergent star Mike Hawthorn for all of the following season. Results, as well as a number of tragedies, pushed Ferrari into selecting foreign drivers for the works team more frequently.
Right: the cutaway of the Ferrari 500 F2 and its rear suspension with the De Dion axle.

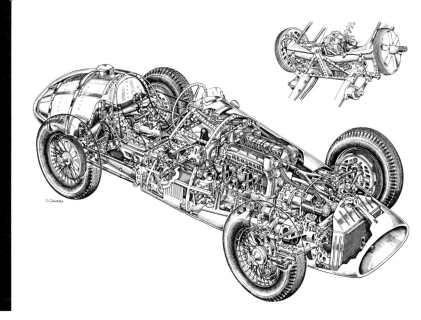

Alberto Ascari: first world champion

26 May 1955, Monza, Ferrari, Ascari. The three world symbols of a motor racing Italy become one in the most tragic of ways. It is lunch time one sunny Thursday, and the Milanese champion asks his friend and "student" Eugenio Castellotti if he could get back to the steering wheel of a racing car and drive the car the young Italian was testing. It was, of course, a Ferrari. Ascari was still affected by the accident of the previous Sunday, when he and his Lancia D 50 suddenly flew into the waters of Monte Carlo harbour. The doctors advised him to rest and his Milan house was undoubtedly the right place. But the call of the race track, the will to cancel out his flight in the Lancia into the Monegasque sea that still disturbs him as he realises that at the Monza circuit, not far from his house, there is a chance to get back to it all. The road

from Corso Sempione in the Milan city centre to the royal park at Monza is short. Like it did not take long for the "maestro" to leave the pits and accelerate away to his destiny. Driving a Ferrari. The story of the greatest Italian post war racing driver and that of Ferrari had been intertwined since Alberto's infancy. His father, Antonio, raced in the years, at the same time and on the same circuits as Enzo Ferrari. The two knew each other when they were young men, linked in different ways to Alfa Romeo and formed a true friendship that ended only with the death of Ascari senior. Years later, when Ferrari became a constructor, even if under the name Auto Avio Costruzione, he would give the then 21 year-old Alberto, son of the unforgettable friend and champion, his debut in the 1940 Mille Miglia.

Formula 1, destined to indelibly mark the 1952-53 seasons: Ferrari-Ascari.
Left, above: the second victory, in the 1952 world championship at Reims; a race that rocketed Ascari right to the top of the world title table.
Below: Ascari waiting for his start in the 1954 Mille Miglia, which he won driving a Lancia D 24. Left: the world champion's driving licence, issued on 2 January 1949, his third season in motor racing after having begun to compete with motorcycles in a distant 1936. Top: the Ferrari single seaters lined up and ready to take to the track for the Grand Prix of Argentina of 18 January 1953. From the left are the cars of Mike Hawthorn, who came fourth, second placed Villoresi, Farina, who retired after he went off causing the deaths of about 10 spectators and the winning Ferrari of Alberto Ascari, who had race number 10 painted on the body.

Opposite: the debut of the 500 F2 at Modena at the end of September 1951 began that day with a victory of the greatest two car-driver names in the history of

following year, even though the world title was still Alfa territory, Ascari was able to win two basic races: on the legendary Nürburgring and at Monza, where he repeated the triumph of 1949. In the meantime, there was the first race and first victory at Modena with the 500 F2, the weapon that would bring the Milanese driver two world titles and the first for Maranello.

In 1952-53 there was no messing about, with Ascari who literally killed the championship, making 11 of the 14 title counters in which he competed his own. He dominated the world title chase as he did the Grands Prix, with that "superb style" of his – the words of Enzo Ferrari – and always in command. But exactly at the culmination of their relationship came, unexpectedly, the divorce. On 30 December 1953, Ferrari announced that the following year he would no longer enjoy the services of the world champion. Ascari moved to Lancia. But for him there would still be a works race with the Rosse of Maranello at the Grand Prix of Italy at Monza. A day in which the spectators went crazy when they saw his car leading the race before he retired. Months later, the track would be the same. The context was changed, it not being a race but simply a private test session. On top of that, it was not Ascari's test session but another driver's, with a car of the opposition. But perhaps destiny wanted Ascari's life to end in a Ferrari on his home track. We shall never know; even today the death of the most successful Italian driver of the last 60 years is still swathed in mystery.

Nine years passed before the two, Enzo Ferrari and Alberto Ascari, would join forces. But the liaison would produce four-and-a-half years of triumph, victories everywhere. Great moments and few disappointments. The first traces of a legend that nobody could foresee at the time.

The start of it all in 1949 was dazzling, with three wins and two third places in five races. The Formula 1 World Championship was born a year later and Ferrari knew he would have to fight it out with Alfa Romeo. He missed the first race of the championship at Silverstone, sending Ascari to win at Mons, Belgium. The first world title clash took place at Monte Carlo with Farina and Fangio driving 158s. Ascari came second behind the Argentinean. No world championship victory in 1950, but the

1956 - Ferrari-Lancia D50
The single seater that came from Turin

In the story of Enzo Ferrari, 1956 was among the most tragic but at the same time a glorious year. On the human front, the loss of his much-loved son Dino at just 24 years of age could certainly not be compensated for by winning two world championships, the drivers' in Formula 1 and the constructors' with his sports racing cars. In addition, during the year considerable controversy surrounded Ferrari in relation to the driver engaged as the number one for that year: the reigning world champion Juan Manuel Fangio.

The Argentinean complained several times during the year of a number of boycotts that he suffered and that forced him to even submit to an examination by a Milanese doctor at the culmination of the clash. The medic declared that Fangio was affected by a form of "reactive neurosis". Regardless, it was Fangio who won the title, doing so in line with the regulations of the period that allowed a driver to take over another car handed to him by a colleague. Exploiting this opportunity, Fangio won the season's opening race in Argentina in Luigi

Musso's car, came second at Monaco in Peter Collins's D 50 and a gentlemanly gesture by the Briton enabled the Argentinean to come second again at Monza to win his fourth world title. Of the seven championship counters, Maranello won five, leaving the remaining two prestigious events, the Grands Prix of Monaco and Monza, to its eternal rival Maserati and Stirling Moss.

As well as in Argentina, Fangio won at Silverstone and the Nürburgring, while Collins took Belgium and France. All thanks to the Lancia D 50, the car used by Ferrari in 1956, which Vittorio Jano and the Turin team had built two years earlier and which had convinced Alberto Ascari to leave Ferrari at the end of 1953. As early as mid-1955, right after the shocking death of Ascari at Monza, all the D 50s and spare parts belonging to Lancia, which was going through a deep financial crisis that forced it to abandon motor sport completely, were ceded to Ferrari; it was due to this patrimony of men and machines that the "court of King Enzo" won its third drivers' title.

A close-up of Juan Manuel Fangio. In his 12 months at Ferrari, the Argentinean driver lived through one of the darkest moments of his career: although he became Formula 1 world champion again, on the human side the disagreements with Enzo Ferrari were at the basis of the separation that led Fangio to reach an agreement with Maserati. Right: Eugenio Castellotti going through Tabac at Monte Carlo. The Principality was the scene of one of the two defeats to which Ferrari was subjected in 1956, both by Stirling Moss. The other was in the Grand Prix of Italy at Monza by the Briton, who crossed the finish line ahead of Fangio on each occasion.

Above: Fangio on his way to victory at Silverstone in the Grand Prix of Great Britain. The Ferrari carried number 1, unusual for races of the period. With the same number, the Argentinean repeated his British success three weeks later at the Nürburgring.

Below: a phase in the last decisive race of 1956, the Grand Prix of Italy at Monza, where Ferrari had entered no fewer than six works cars, despite the fact that the title was an in-house battle between its drivers. Castellotti is in the lead, shadowed by Musso.

1958 - 246 F1
They begin to speak English

Three close-ups of great drivers who all died within a few months of each other. Above left: Mike Hawthorn, who already had health problems, and who lost his life in a banal road accident in January 1959, a few weeks after becoming the F1 world champion and having announced his retirement from the sport. Below, left: Luigi Musso flew off the track in his Ferrari during the Grand Prix of France in July 1958; his injuries were fatal. The same happened to Peter Collins at the Nürburgring a month later, the driver shown here next to his friend and great photographer Bernard Cahier.
In the photograph top right, a moment in the Grand Prix of Buenos Aires of 2 February, an unusually wet race in the normally torrid South American summer. Wolfgang von Trips precedes Musso in a Dino 246, the car with which Ferrari competed in the 1958 F1 season.
Centre, right: one of the last pictures of Collins, on the 22 kilometre Nürburgring on that fatal 3 August 1958.

Ferrari began this ninth year of the Formula One World Championship with the new Dino 246, which took over from the 801, descendent of the now outdated Lancia D 50, which first saw the light of day in 1954. It did so without realising that, in a short time; there would literally be an epoch-making technical turnaround with the engines being installed behind the cockpit and relative rear traction. The point would not be taken by Maranello until after the victories of the little Cooper-Climaxes of Stirling Moss in Argentina and Maurice Trintignant in Monaco, the first two world championship rounds. With Maserati out of the way after its 1957 world title win with Fangio, Vanwall joined Cooper as another British contender for the world titles. The English newcomer entered the sport forcefully giving first Stirling Moss in Holland and then Tony Brooks in Belgium the opportunity of keeping Ferrari out of the 1958 title chase.

But in the subsequent summer classics two Ferrari victories were chalked up in France and Britain: Mike Hawthorn won at Reims on the day Luigi Musso tragically lost his life and at Silverstone it was the turn of Peter Collins to take the win. But in Germany two weeks later, death struck again when gentleman and hero of Monza in 1956, Peter Collins, crashed and died. The championship continued to be unresolved right up to the last race in Morocco, with Hawthorn a heartbeat from the title and Moss as the only adversary able to beat him on points. At Casablanca Hawthorn's second enabled him to beat his countryman – also thanks to Phil Hill, who let himself be overtaken in that crucial finale – by a single point. In the previous race at Monza, Vanwall, meanwhile, won the first Constructors' Cup which, under various denominations and different regulations, still renders honour to today's best Formula 1 constructors.

Two pictures showing Luigi Musso in a couple of world championship races in 1958. Right: the Italian going through the old station corner at Monte Carlo. Below: driving the Dino 246, making its debut on the Buenos Aires circuit. Musso came second in both Argentina and Monaco and, due to those results, went to the top of the championship table. He scored no points in the subsequent rounds at Zandvoort and Spa and in the fifth race on the Reims road circuit he was involved in a fatal accident while trying to overtake Mike Hawthorn. It was in that country that the Briton won his only GP of the season, which remained open until the last GP at Casablanca, Morocco. The Briton came second behind his rival Stirling Moss, but was still able to take the title by one point.

Alfa Romeo, Mercedes and not only…

As motor sport history tells us, Nino Farina and Juan Manuel Fangio won the first Formula 1 World Championships for drivers. They did so at the wheel of Alfa Romeos; a sort of mother, to express the point using that term of endearment uttered by Enzo Ferrari. But still, these two post war champions competed to add to the list of races won by Ferrari after leaving the Milanese constructor. The Argentinean even won the 1956 title in his one controversial season at the court of Maranello. The five times world champion did not give up even after his divorce from Ferrari, beating his old team with the disliked Maserati: the supreme snub. The Scuderia rose again and enabled Mike Hawthorn to win the first of a long series of world titles achieved by the subjects of His Majesty

King Enzo, who soon became the leader in Grand Prix victories and world titles. But the British F1 driver par excellence between the Fifties and Sixties was Stirling Moss, a king without a crown; although he came second four times in succession between 1955 and 1958, he never won the F1 World Championship for drivers. Moss competed against the Ferraristi for many seasons, beating them or losing to them, but beyond the results, the great admiration Enzo Ferrari had for the Briton never diminished, so much so that he most certainly would have wanted him in his team. Perhaps because Hawthorn showed him that overseas drivers had something more to give than all the others. Finished with the Argentineans, with the Brazilians and

saries and paraded one after the other across the finish line after 500 kilometres of racing. Car number 20 was driven by the ageing Karl Kling and he was preceded by Juan Manuel Fangio who, in the photograph top, left is shown in the cockpit of his Alfa Romeo "Alfetta" 158 of 1950. Underneath is a moment in the 1957 Grand Prix of Argentina; a race that only saw Ferrari and its bitter "enemy" Maserati at the start. Fangio won and is shown bottom left behind Moss, both in Maserati 250 Fs, the most successful car in the Modena constructor's history and the only one to have given the manufacturer an F1 world title. Above: a close-up of Stirling Moss. The London driver raced with nine different marques and was able to win world championship Grands Prix with five of them.
Below: Jack Brabham, winner of the 1959 and 1960 F1 world titles with the revolutionary rear engined Cooper T 51 and T 53.

The entry of Mercedes-Benz into Formula 1 in July 1954 had a devastating effect on its rival constructors.
Opposite: Reims on 4 July the debutante German W 196 lapped all their adver-

French still to come, the Italians tragically gone, the British would have become the "master race" and the triad of Graham Hill, Jim Clark and John Surtees divided up the races and titles of the early Sixties between them. But if Hill and Clark were respected rivals of the Prancing Horse, Big John, already a seven times motorcycle racing champion, built a large part of his legend at Maranello at that 1964 Grand Prix of Mexico City. Then he left, too, returning to the track to beat Ferrari. And he did with Cooper, worse still equipped with the hated Maserati engine. Then he even beat the Scuderia at Monza in a Honda: the first warning that the Nipponese empire was on its way to Formula 1 in various waves of attack.

1961 - 156 F1
The first rear engined Ferrari world championship car

The International Federation had already decided some time earlier to bring in the new cubic capacity of just 1,500 cc for 1961. Although losing the opening race in Monte Carlo, won by Stirling Moss in a Lotus, Ferrari was the constructor that best interpreted the new regulation. It did it so well that it won the world constructors' championship for the first time at the fifth of the season's nine races, the Grand Prix of Great Britain. The 156 F1, designed by engineer Carlo Chiti, wiped the floor with rivals

Above: Phil Hill's 156 F1, who came third at Monte Carlo.
Left: Giancarlo Baghetti during practice in his home Grand Prix, which ended for him on the 14th lap with engine trouble. After his win at Reims, the Italian was unable to repeat that success and his career faded into anonymity in the years that followed.
Opposite: the unfortunate Wolfgang von Trips. For years a faithful disciple of the Italian team, in the summer of 1961 the baron, who came from Cologne, was more than ever on his way to the F1 world championship. Then came the terrible tragedy at Monza.

Porsche, Cooper, Lotus and BRM, permitting its lead drivers, American Phil Hill and German nobleman Wolfgang von Trips, to compete against each other for the world drivers' title in the last two rounds, the Grands Prix of Italy and the United States.
At Monza, the superiority of Ferrari already appeared significant in qualifying, with the first four places on the grid; sixth was Giancarlo Baghetti in a Rossa. Tragedy struck on the second lap of the race: a collision between Jim Clark's Lotus and the Ferrari of von Trips, the German driver and his car flying into the netting behind which were the spectators. The driver and 14 members of the crowd died in that disaster. Phil Hill won the race, ignoring the condition of his friend and, with his only rival for the title now dead, winning the F1 World Championship for drivers.
After the World Sports Car Championship and the F1 title, a sad epilogue, Ferrari decided to suspend its works F1 activity and did not travel to the last Grand Prix at Watkins Glen, the home-country of the new world champion. At the end of the year, the company made a gesture that was as clamorous as it was unexpected by firing eight of its managers on the spot, which included the trusted Motor Sport Director Romolo Tavoni and the well-respected designer Carlo Chiti.
And that was not the only important decision carried out during the year. After an awful sequence of deaths in recent seasons involving young, talented Italian drivers at the wheel of cars from Maranello, in 1961 Ferrari went back to assigning his single seaters to an Italian, choosing Giancarlo Baghetti; but he did so his own way, ensuring other teams enter the young Milanese while the company provided all the official support. Baghetti did not disappoint, either, winning on his debut in the F1 world championship race at Reims after having already won the first two events in which he competed at Syracuse and Naples, which were not valid for the world title.

1964 - 158 F1
A car of the English school

Four years earlier Ferrari converted to rear engines for its single seaters on the heels of the British constructors. The 158 appeared in 1964 and meant that Maranello was on the same level as its overseas rivals for the first time. It was built of a semi-monocoque in aluminium panels and was powered by a new-concept eight cylinder engine.

The team was limited to two works drivers: Briton John Surtees and Italian Lorenzo Bandini. They would be joined at Monza by Ludovico Scarfiotti, while for the delicate Mexican race at the end of the season a 156 was also placed at the disposal of Pedro Rodriguez. For the two last races Ferrari, in open war with the Italian Federation because it did not homologate the 250 LM in the Grand Touring category, entered its cars in the blue and white colours of importer Luigi Chinetti's Scuderia N.A.R.T., turning its back on the classic red to send a clear message to the offending organisation. Three victories in 10 races for the Italian Scuderia; after Surtees won at the Nürburgring Bandini did likewise at the first Grand Prix of Austria to be valid for the world championship, followed by a Surtees win again in the anxiously awaited Italian GP at Monza.

With his triumph in the Grand Prix of Italy and the simultaneous retirement of his nearest rivals, Surtees was back in the reckoning for the drivers' world title. After a second place in the United States, Surtees was to fight it out for the championship with Scotland's reigning champion Jim Clark in a Lotus, and fellow countryman Graham Hill in a BRM – the car in which he won the title two years earlier – in Mexico City. The race was packed with drama: from Bandini's shunt into the back of Hill's car, which forced the Briton into a pit stop, to the retirement of Clark, undisputed leader from the start, a few kilometres from the end. Surtees, who was second behind ex-Ferrari driver Dan Gurney, and his Italian

team mate avoided attacking the American, knowing second place would bring him enough points with which to win the world championship. With that second, Maranello also won the constructors' championship for the second time, completing a season that began negatively with only one podium finish in four races.

It was not long before the start of the GP of Italy and John Surtees (top) is getting ready, surrounded by men of Ferrari. The British driver, who was not much more than 30 at the time, had already enjoyed an outstanding career on motorcycles, winning 6 world championships in the second half of the '50s. Having taken up car racing in 1960, he joined Ferrari 3 years later and immediately took centre stage. Below: Lorenzo Bandini at Monte Carlo, where he retired with gearbox problems, although he was eventually classified 10th. The Italian driver's results were poor in the first part of the season.

Above: John Surtees taking the "new world" corner in the Grand Prix of France at Reims. He retired for the third time in four races. Below, right: the future world champion following the Brabham of Dan Gurney at Monza. The race was dominated by a duel between these two drivers, who exchanged the lead 27 times until mechanical problems slowed the American, leaving the way clear for Surtees.

Below, left: Ferrari mechanics refuelling a 158 during a test session that Ferrari usually ran at Monza before the Grand Prix of Italy. In 1964, too, Ferrari was especially keen to win its home Grand Prix, taking a new car powered by a 12-cylinder engine to the circuit for Bandini. But the Milanese driver preferred to race the tried and tested 158, postponing the debut of the new car to the North American race.

1975 - 312 T
"T" as in Triumph

Top: Niki Lauda on his way to victory at Paul Ricard. His triumph in France consolidated his lead in the world championship: he only needed a few more points in subsequent races to win the title before season's end and celebrate the return of the Formula 1 World Championship for drivers to Ferrari 11 years after John Surtees's success.

Below: Clay Regazzoni's helmet and gloves; basic components in a search for safety which, in the mid-Seventies, became an increasingly prominent issue among drivers. The active contribution of Jackie Stewart first of all, then Niki Lauda later, raised the safeguard level of the active and passive safety of the drivers in case of an accident.

To return to the top of Formula 1, Ferrari definitively renounced endurance racing with prototypes at the start of 1974. The results were encouraging, with Maranello once again taking the top places during that first year as a result of three wins, of which two were by new arrival Niki Lauda, even if Clay Regazzoni lost the world title in the last race in the United States to Brazilian Emerson Fittipaldi.

For 1975, Maranello fielded a new single seater with an equally new transverse gearbox. From that comes the letter "T" in the designation of the car, designed by engineer Mauro Forghieri, and a car that used the flat V12 erroneously called a boxer for the sixth consecutive season.

But the season did not get off the ground in an ideal way. The team started by taking the outmoded previous year's 312 B3 to South America, waiting for the new car to become available for the third race in the world championship. But after four Grands Prix neither of the drivers had even scored a podium finish. But Lauda won at Monte Carlo and the races that followed clearly showed the 312 T's great technical superiority, together with the explosive talent of the Austrian driver.

The adversaries that, race after race, tried to beat Niki were always different; a factor that favoured Lauda in the end in his sprint to the title, which he won on an important day at the Grand Prix of Italy at Monza. His team mate Regazzoni won the race with the 26 year-old Austrian third behind the second placed Fittipaldi, who was soundly beaten for the title. With the points scored at Monza, Ferrari also won the constructors' championship, which brought to a close a long drought that lasted 11 years both for the drivers' and constructors' crowns, the latter of which Enzo Ferrari coveted the most as it went to the best team. As well as the technical staff and the drivers in the achievement of this historic result there is the direction of a

man who would later take on a fundamental role in the history of Ferrari: Luca Cordero di Montezemolo. His presence in the pits was always essential: he acted as a kind of lightning conductor when the absence of results had to be justified, but at the same time he indicated the right road to take in the field in order to achieve the team's fixed objectives.

After a period of oblivion, the genius of engineer Mauro Forghieri (pictured left) returned to the F1 spotlight with the Ferrari "T" series.
Below: Clay Regazzoni, runner-up in the 1974 world championship, was unable to repeat that performance in 1975 and had to accept team orders to help Niki Lauda to win the title. With the mathematical certainty that it would arrive at Monza, he was left free to run his own race, winning before a public that had already acclaimed him five years earlier. In the black and white picture is the rear end of the 312 T during testing at Monza. At the time, an articulated lorry was used to carry the two racing cars plus the essential tools with which to gather information on the track.
Below, right: Lauda on 28 March 1976 at the first Grand Prix of Long Beach. Previously, the Austrian had won in Brazil and South Africa, but in the Californian city victory went to Regazzoni, a success that marked the end of the glorious 312 T, that being the last race in which the outstanding car from Maranello competed.

Above, left: Clay Regazzoni in discussion with motor sport director Luca Cordero di Montezemolo. The young team boss immediately showed his organisation skills, which made him a man fundamental to the results of the team. His predilection for Niki Lauda was never declared, but it would be basic to the Austrian conquering the world championship at the end of the year.
Above, right: Prince Rainier and his wife Princess Grace have just presented the winner's cup to Lauda, who brought to an end Ferrari's 20 years of no victories in the Principality: a Rossa had not won in Monaco since Maurice Trintignant in 1955. Below: the Austrian in the narrow pit lane of his home Grand Prix at Zeltweg. The race went into the history books as the only success of Vittorio Brambilla. The Italian drove to victory through a severe storm that hit the Styria circuit before the start. Lauda came sixth, but that only gave him half a point due to the early suspension of the race. Ironically, nine years later, the Austrian won his third world title in a McLaren by half a point, beating his team mate Alain Prost.

Niki Lauda, from "Computer" to Champion

Like it or not, few drivers have left a tangible mark on motor racing that goes beyond the role of honour, of their passing through the history of motor racing. But one of them is Andreas Nikolaus Lauda, known to everyone as Niki. There are many who were not exactly crazy about him during his years at Ferrari, even though they supported the Italian constructor; they expected something that summer of 1977 that many people saw as betrayal, turning his back on those who, Enzo Ferrari at the top of the list, had done a great deal for him. Few, however, realised that his behaviour and his sincerity were a concrete way of raising the level of this much-loved sport, always increasingly popular yet still highly dangerous.

Lauda began his Ferrari adventure during his third year in Formula 1 after two seasons at March and BRM without much success, but probably with a great deal of hidden potential. For many he was an unknown, a young Austrian with buck teeth and hair tending towards blond. His physical appearance was changed by a terrible accident at the Nürburgring on 1 August 1976, without imagining that in a few months the whole world of racing would realise that Lauda was not only a talented driver. That he clearly confirmed in his refusal that led him to say no to Ferrari when the Commendatore offered him yet another contract. First it was Ascari, then Surtees and perhaps other drivers about whose names there is no proof. But two world titles were enough to understand in which company to place the Austrian. That of the great champions.

His four years with the Rossa were those of the relaunch, of victories, of being unbeatable, of the tragedy that immediately changed the scenario and, without wanting to, also that of the future of the young man of Austrian bourgeoisie. In his first year, together with the pleasant and jovial Clay Regazzoni, Niki seemed like a cold calculator and that is why he was baptised The Computer. He did not win the title; in part, he made Regazzoni lose it. Year two, with the complicity of a car called the 312 T, he cancelled out 11 years of world championship defeats. But 1976, the third of the Lauda era, was his year, even if the name James Hunt appeared under the heading "world champion" in the roles of honour of all the books. Years later, Michael Schumacher travelled along the same road, made up of races dominated, Grands Prix won, undisputed pole positions and a whole lot more. Many, quite rightly, shouted great champion. Until mid-summer 1976 the same thing happened to Lauda. Then, suddenly, as only accidents can determine, from the podium of one circuit he passed to a hospital ward. God did not want him to end up as an obituary. Perhaps God did not particularly love Lauda, but for certain he did not need the Austrian at the time. Fortunately, things went differently and many, once again rightly, called out for a miracle. Six weeks later, Niki returned to Formula 1 at Monza in the cockpit of his Ferrari. He was a protagonist again, if only for the fact that he was there. He lost his title in Japan, and for many also some esteem. But the man and the champion did not care about controversy and a year

The 312 T2 of 1976 was the ideal car for the continuation of Niki Lauda's career, the car that enabled him to win his second consecutive Formula 1 World Championship.
Opposite: the Austrian driver was so much at ease at the wheel of the Ferrari that he was always able to take a podium place in the first part of the season, with the exception of the French GP at Paul Ricard. With the imminent German race on 1 August on the difficult Nürburgring Lauda, having come second in qualifying, predicted the concrete possibility of him obtaining his umpteenth positive result. That is one

of the subjects that occupied the Ferrari staff (top right) comprising the two drivers, engineer Antonio Tomagni and the motor sport director Daniele Audetto. The picture, taken in the pits of the hellish 'Ring, is one of the last of the unscarred face of the Austrian driver. From that day on, his appearance would be forever disfigured by the blazing full fuel tanks of his 312 T2, after the car had flown off the track during the early laps. There would follow days of anxiety, with the driver hovering between life and death. Then, after only a few weeks, Lauda made his courageous and historic return at Monza.

later, in 1977 in Japan, Lauda could have avoided returning. The world championship re-consigned him to the Scuderia that paid him before the end of the season, and he could permit himself to challenge Ferrari in the future without having to bow down.
Two years at Brabham at the court of Bernie Ecclestone, the "English assembler", in a car powered by an Alfa Romeo engine, as if he wanted to be disrespectful to Ferrari, except then also acknowledging the increasingly influential British boss, with whom he would compete in two world championships in 1978-79. Then he caught the first plane out and left, but also here the scene is not a standard one, because the aeroplanes are his, belonging to a company he created.
Meanwhile, Jody Scheckter made the triumphs of Niki move from the showcase of Maranello, substituting them with his own. The man who took his place, a young Canadian, makes the worship disappear from crowds of red tifosi. Gilles Villeneuve was not, and unfortunately would never be, like Lauda. But…
Two years later, the return via the court of another British boss, Ron Dennis, who with Lauda's comeback, would lay the first serious cornerstone of the future McLaren empire. At the third race it was already victory and two years later it was the title again. The third. Another last year of racing, then retirement. This time for good. From the cockpit, but not from a world that would see him as a McLaren, Ferrari and Jaguar manager, and that, even today, knows that his are simple but not banal words. Like his story.

1976 - 312 T2
An incredibile season

For 1976, the International Federation introduced a number of new regulations, among which the most evident was the abolition of the large air intakes above the driver's head. In the meantime, Ferrari honed its new weapon, the 312 T2, a natural evolution of the T. The "old" car was still unbeatable and won the first three races of the season in Brazil, South Africa and

The starting grid at Zandvoort: Clay Regazzoni concentrating on the imminent race. At his left is new motor sport director Daniele Audetto, while standing behind the car in a white shirt is Giulio Borsani, the great mechanic and the Swiss driver's right hand man, in his last season at Ferrari.

Long Beach. Then the T2 took to the track for the fourth round, the Grand Prix of Spain, but with this race the Formula 1 story entered into a new era, made up of protests, disqualifications, tribunals and appeals. The victory of Britain's James Hunt in the McLaren M23 was only made official after a number of weeks to the detriment of Niki Lauda who won, after technical verification carried out on Hunt's McLaren a few hours after the end of the race.

Something similar, but with the roles reversed, happened at the Grand Prix of Great Britain, but the key moment of the season took place at the Nürburgring when Lauda, who was on his way to the world title, was the victim of his horrendous crash that left him hovering between life and death. The Austrian was confined to a hospital bed, but planned his return and was back racing three Grands Prix later at Monza, convinced that he could retain his world crown in the remaining rounds of the series. The battle for world honours continued with Hunt, who had scored more precious points in the meantime.

And that is how they arrived at the last race in Japan, with Lauda still firmly in the lead but with the Briton mathematically ready to exploit a title chance that was considered unthinkable three months earlier.

The well-known drama that took place at the foot of Mount Fuji took away a much deserved title from the reigning Austrian world champion who, in deciding not to race in the downpour showed a side of his character that not everyone, Enzo Ferrari at the top of the list, understood or accepted.

Lauda's team mate in this dramatic 1976, Clay Regazzoni, had been reconfirmed but was never in with a chance of the title; at the end of the year was "deprived" of his place in the team by Carlos Reutemann. The Argentinean had been hurriedly whisked to Monza to replace the convalescent Lauda and then, with the sudden return of Niki, was entered in a third T2.

Above, left: Clay Regazzoni and Niki Lauda at the presentation of the 312 T2. Next to them, Enzo Ferrari is conscious of having brought to life another winning single seater. However, the T2 had to be modified before its official debut in that the Federation regarded the end plates positioned in front of the front wheels as illegal as they also incorporated the brake air intake.

Above, centre: Lauda on the Friday of the Grand Prix of Italy during the few laps he drove in heavy rain. The Austrian was still recovering from his Nürburgring accident 40 days earlier, as the picture top right shows. Despite the pain, he wanted to compete at Monza in an attempt to ward off an attack from James Hunt on his world championship lead. At Monza, the Englishman went off, while Lauda came fourth. But the

nightmare of the rain also descended on the final race in Japan. Lauda, with a decision that made history, refused to continue the race, saying goodbye to the chance of winning a title, which ended up in the hands of James Hunt and McLaren. Above, right centre: Clay Regazzoni at the Spanish debut of the 312 T2; a race that saw the Swiss finish out of the points. Below: Lauda slows due to the sudden suspension of the race at

Brands Hatch after a starting accident involving Hunt's McLaren, among others. For the re-start, the Briton turned up in a spare car and won the race, but the manoeuvre was considered illegal and after a number of days victory was assigned to Lauda. At that moment, with eight podium places in nine races to his credit, nobody imagined that the Austrian would lose the title at the end of the year.

Despite the unthinkable epilogue to the drivers' battle for the title, Ferrari meritoriously took the constructors' championship again at the penultimate race. In 1977, Lauda and Reutemann became a solid team, which continued to produce the results achieved in the two previous years. By mid-season, the Ferrari drivers were in a position to battle it out for the world championship against Mario Andretti in the Lotus and the newcomer Wolf, its car driven by Jody Scheckter, their remaining only rivals. Lauda competed in the second half of the season with great intelligence by scoring five consecutive podium finishes, culminating with a second at Monza. That result gave Maranello its third consecutive constructors' world championship, but soon just before came the shock announcement of the divorce between Niki and Ferrari.

In the subsequent race at Watkins Glen, Lauda was content with a fourth place, which enabled him to score enough points with which to win his second world title of his career.

On his return from the American race he announced that he would not compete in the last two Grands Prix of the year in Canada and Japan, leaving his car free, which Ferrari assigned it to an unknown driver. His name was Gilles Villeneuve.

Niki Lauda in the 1977 312 T2. The car was the natural evolution of the one that had dominated the previous season. Among the few modifications were the two Naca air intakes at the sides of the cockpit, which were bigger on the T in 1976. This umpteenth development of the 312 was of the calibre of its predecessor.

Above, left: Carlos Reutemann in the Grand Prix of Spain, in which he came second. Below: the Argentinean driver again, this time preceding his team mate Lauda at Monte Carlo, the Austrian second and the Argentinean third. Lauda would move ahead of the Ferrari newcomer by just two points. In the remaining nine races fought out for the world championship under the same roof, Reutemann would never again do better than Lauda with the exception of the third place in Sweden. Right: Niki in the pits. On his right is engineer Mauro Forghieri, chief technician and architect of the Ferrari victories in the second half of the Seventies.

1979 - 312 T4
The last series T world champion

The 1978 season drew to a close with the victory of Canadian Gilles Villeneuve on his home track at Montreal, but the season was not the best, despite five Grand Prix wins out of 16 races, four of which achieved with the 312 T3. This latest Maranello creation could do nothing to stop the Lotus 78 and 79 of Mario Andretti and Ronnie Peterson and the fugitive Niki Lauda in a Brabham–Alfa Romeo was passed by Carlos Reutemann in the world championship at the last race, the Argentinean leaving Ferrari at the end of the season. With the new year on the horizon, Ferrari introduced South African Jody Scheckter as the man to take over from Reutemann and went to the third race of the season with the 312 T4, which started life at the top with two 1.2s in South Africa and at Long Beach. Both races were won by Gilles Villeneuve, who increasingly worked his way into the good graces of Enzo Ferrari and the infinite multitude of the team's tifosi. But as the season progressed, it was clear that Scheckter was the more concrete driver in terms of results, even if less spectacular. That enabled him to top the drivers' world championship table on the eve of Monza, which was anxiously

Left: an intense close-up of Jody Scheckter, ready to speed off to a pole position or a victory in his 312 T4. Above: the South African in the Grand Prix of Great Britain at Silverstone where he came fifth on the day that Williams scored its historic first F1 victory. Scheckter joined Ferrari at the end of 1978 known as an impulsive person due mostly to the accidents he caused at the start of his career. His first race for Ferrari in Argentina ended with a multiple accident at the first corner, after which his more mature approach meant he became involved in fewer crashes.

awaited by the Italian public. In the preceding race at Zandvoort, the irrepressible Villeneuve once again showed his indomitable character by covering a complete lap of the Dutch circuit with a dislodged rear wheel dangling from his car before reaching the pits and being forced to retire. Scheckter came second in Holland, so at that point success in the Grand Prix of Italy could assign both titles to Ferrari, provided the two Maranello drivers came first and second, Jody leading.

Villeneuve obeyed team orders and "escorted" his friend and team mate to the finish line, enabling the Italian constructor to close triumphantly one of the most glorious days in its long history. Villeneuve took second place in his home Grand Prix and won at Watkins Glen, certain that the following year he

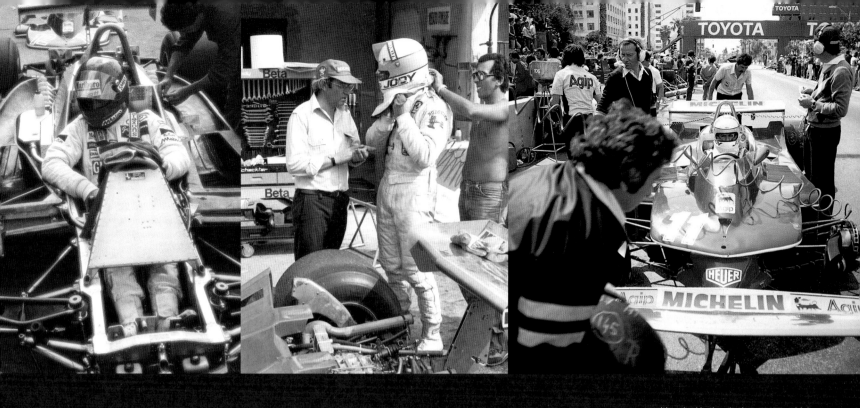

Above: three pictures of the men of Ferrari, who "attend" to the two drivers of that unforgettable 1979. The season began in Buenos Aires with a double retirement for the "old" 312 T3s. In the meantime Ligier's star was born which, with victories by Jacques Laffite in Argentina and the next race in Brazil. At Interlagos, Ferrari was defended by its drivers who took the last two points positions, but the fact that both had been lapped made it obvious that the T3 was outdated.

The arrival of the new car overturned the situation, with Ferrari becoming a winning team. Positive results began to arrive and continued throughout the season, even if the win of the Renault Turbo in France showed everyone the road to take was that of the turbocharged engine. At Dijon, however, Gilles Villeneuve Below, competing at Monte Carlo) stole the race together with René Arnoux with a duel in the closing stages, which remains one of the great spectacles of all time in motor racing. Even today that 1 July 1979 is remembered more for the continual overtaking manoeuvres and tyre banging of the two French speakers than for the first victory of a turbo engine in Formula 1.

would be repaid for what he did and, therefore, placed in a position of being able to win the Formula 1 World Championship in 1980. Unfortunately, the 312 T5 was not a good car and the season would be a negative one for the Canadian. It was just as bad for Scheckter, as he was unable to defend his title and he retired from motor racing physically at the end of the season after having done so psychologically during the year.

A picture of the Gilles Villeneuve's 312 T4 during a winning performance in the last Grand Prix of the season at Watkins Glen. The Canadian was finally free of team orders after the Italian success, which gave the world drivers' championship to

Jody Scheckter, who finished second on his home track and in the U.S. event. Everything suggested a golden 1980 for Villeneuve, but instead he had to wait until the 1981 Grand Prix of Monaco to return to the podium of a world title race.

Formula 1 was in continuous technical and sporting evolution, but Ferrari was not always on top of its game as was the case 20 years earlier with the belated adoption of rear engines. Instead, Maranello has always had an eye for aerodynamics, having installed a rudimentary wind tunnel in the early Sixties and at the end of that decade by introducing the first rear wing.

At the time, race weekends were still the best opportunities to experiment with the right solutions. Until the Seventies, the only data that could be consulted was often lap times. An example of this research in the field can be seen in the two photographs above left of Jody Scheckter during practice at Monte Carlo, where he tried two different rear wings. In the race, both he and his team mate Villeneuve chose the "advanced" units and set the two fastest times in qualifying.

The South African achieved success, but an accident caused Villeneuve's retirement. Below: a moment in the Monegasque Grand Prix, with the two Ferraris being tailed by Alan Jones in a Williams. The duel all those years ago brings us back to the present with a thought that is not technical but commercial. It was the era of the Arabian sponsors in Formula 1, thanks to the British team. For years, Frank Williams received finance from various Middle East sheiks, while at the beginning of this century the Italian team is a financial partner of the various Emirates. The picture above right shows the finish of the Grand Prix of France with Villeneuve second, preceding his rival and friend Réne Arnoux ahead of him in a Renault by little more than two tenths of a second.

The era of the great champions

Two months after John Surtees won the Formula 1 World Championship, the sport welcomed the debut of a driver who would leave his indelible mark on the sporting and political history of F1. From Scotland came Jackie Stewart, who competed in the maximum formula for nine years after that New Year's Day in 1965. In that period of time, Ferrari only won nine races out of over 100 Grands Prix against 27 victories by the Scotsman, who also won 3 world championships. Maranello won no titles at all. Ken Tyrrell's "pupil" having left the sport, the shining star of the great Brazilian Emerson Fittipaldi rose high in the sky. With him the accounts, the real ones, were equal. A title ripped away from Clay Regazzoni in 1974 and a defeat a year later at the hands of

Niki Lauda. Fittipaldi drove a McLaren and from then on rivalry exploded onto the scene between these two teams, about which the final chapters must still be written. They were Ferrari and McLaren: two names to which Lauda owes much, perhaps everything, certainly his three F1 world titles. But before McLaren, the public enemy number one was called Lotus. From the times of Jim Clark to one of the many ex-Ferrari drivers Mario Andretti. After Colin Chapman's Lotus left the scene, its place was taken by a small organisation run by a shrewd man who knows Italy and its language well. His name is Frank Williams. These were the years in which the talented South African Jody Scheckter aspired to the title of world number one. He tried with

Jim Clark absorbed on the opposite page, while his mechanics adjust his Lotus. The Scottish champion had tied his career to Colin Chapman's team alone, with which he won his two world titles. Opposite, top right: another intense look from Graham Hill. Like Clark, the Briton was one of Chapman's preferred drivers, but apart from winning the championship with the designer's cars in 1968, he had done the same thing with BRM six years earlier. Below: Jackie Stewart's Tyrrell 003 of 1971, the year literally dominated by the newborn British team. On this page: Emerson Fittipaldi's 1975 McLaren M23 carrying the number one of the world champion on its nose; a practice required by the Federation and inaugurated that year.

Above, right: a moment of relax in the Brazilian pits for the only two drivers who managed to win the world title in the second half of the Seventies, interspersed with those of Ferrari. Two years later, James Hunt in 1976 and Mario Andretti were among the best drivers of that golden era of F1. Centre, left: Nelson Piquet talking to the ingenious Brabham designer of the period, Gordon Murray. The Brazilian battled with Williams (below with Alan Jones in 1979) before joining the British team and winning the title in 1987.

McLaren, Tyrrell with four and six wheels and with the millionaire John Wolf. Nothing, just great races. Then he won the title with Ferrari in 1979, but his team mate Gilles Villeneuve dazzled the eyes of the fans. It was also the year in which Alan Jones started to win and the following season, in the midst of a Ferrari technical debacle, gave Frank Williams and Patrick Head their first world championship. The next year could have been the stuff of champions for the English team, which now had ample resources from the Arab world. There was not long to go and it seemed that the title would be won by another ex-Ferrari driver Carlos Reutemann, but the victor turned out to be Nelson Piquet. The son of the Brazilian ex-Minister of Health would never make his way to Maranello. Indeed, he would have hard words to say about Ferrari. Harder still was his success on the track, for he won three F1 world championships. Titles that arrived after battles with two important rivals: Nigel Mansell and especially Alain Prost. When they were beaten by the standard bearer of Bernie Ecclestone's Brabham first and then Williams, nobody imagined that Mansell and Prost would drive the Rosse together in 1990. And certainly no-one imagined that, once they had left Ferrari, each would win the title.

1982 - 126 C2
Title in the darkest year

Top: Gilles Villeneuve and Didier Pironi, the two drivers with whom Ferrari began its season number 43 in the Formula One World Championship. A tragic and glorious year in which both Ferraristi were involved in horrific accidents. The Canadian the misunderstanding during the Grand Prix of Belgium with Jochen Mass was fatal. Misunderstanding with Alain Prost was also at the root of severe injuries to Pironi's legs during the Grand Prix of Germany, ending his motor racing career. Below: Patrick Tambay and Mario Andretti, who replaced the two unfortunate drivers at different times.

A little more than a year after Renault, Ferrari took to the road of turbo charged engines, which was opened by the French constructor in 1977. The results were close-fought and great moments like victories at Monte Carlo and in Spain in 1981 alternated with sonorous technical and image defeats. But in 1982, Ferrari built a car that proved interesting, the 126 C2. Already a member of the team for a year with a confirmed Gilles Villeneuve was Frenchman Didier Pironi, a well-experienced driver who did not show he was of the level of his Canadian team mate in 1981. The 1982 season was one of the most tragic for Maranello. During qualifying for the fifth race of the year at Zolder, Belgium, the team lost Villeneuve forever in an accident due to a misunderstanding as he was overtaking Jochen Mass in a March. Two weeks earlier, he had competed in the Grand Prix of San Marino at Imola and Ferrari, due to the absence of the British teams, achieved an easy 1-2 on their home circuit. There was a useless battle between the two Ferrari drivers in the final stages of the race – despite a signal from the pits to maintain positions when Gilles was in the lead – but first across the finish line was Pironi with Villeneuve second. A situation that enraged Villeneuve and reacted considerable bad blood between two, so much so that the Canadian swore he would never speak to Didier again and arrived at the next fatal race in Belgium in a state of tremendous internal agitation. The world championship continued after the Zolder tragedy, various drivers winning the remaining Grands Prix. That situation was a help to Pironi, who took the lead in the title chase, but in early August he was also involved in a serious accident while qualifying for the Grand Prix of Germany. His legs were so badly fractured that he was unable to compete for the rest of the season. Ferrari had already replaced Villeneuve with Patrick Tambay and now found itself in the unpleasant situation of having the best car but without its

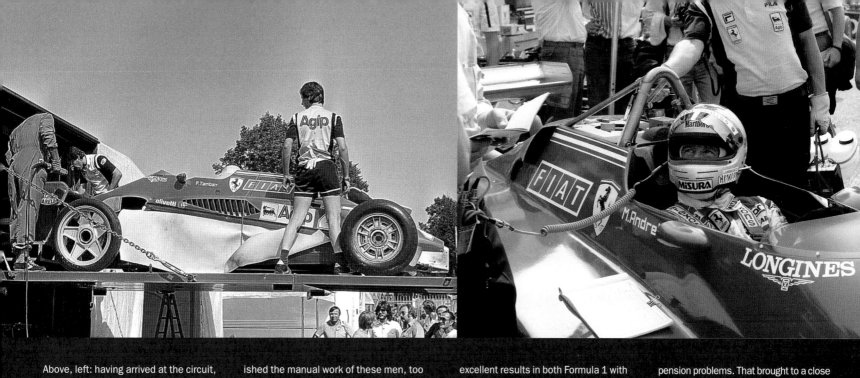

Above, left: having arrived at the circuit, the Ferrari mechanics begin to unload the cars. The behind-the-scenes work of the men in the pits has always been an important element in the success or otherwise in motor sport. At the start of the Eighties, though, the arrival of electronics in the world of Formula 1 partly diminished the manual work of these men, too often turning them into mere executors of choices dictated by a computer.

Above, right: Mario Andretti talking to Ferrari technicians during a pit stop at the Grand Prix of Italy. The Italo-American had already been a Ferrari driver at the beginning of the Seventies, when he achieved excellent results in both Formula 1 with the 312 B and sports car racing driving the 512 S first and then the glorious 312 PB. He was recalled to the team a few days before free practice to take Pironi's place in the Italian Grand Prix at Monza where he took pole and came third, but he retired from the next race at Las Vegan with suspension problems. That brought to a close Andretti's second sojourn at Ferrari.

Below: the last Grand Prix driven by Gilles Villeneuve was the San Marino at Imola on 25 April 1982. The Canadian came second, which sparked off a storm that has not come to an end after many years.

drivers being able to fight for the world title. The German race was won by Tambay, while the great Andretti was brought over from America to take the place of Pironi. The Italo-American champion immediately showed his class, taking pole position and third place in his debut at the wheel of the 126 C2 at Monza, but especially scoring points which became decisive in enabling Ferrari to win the F1 World Championship for constructors again.

Below, large picture: Mario Andretti takes the flag in the Grand Prix of Italy at Monza, with the trackside spectators ready to burst onto the track. Below, left: Didier Pironi, the unfortunate protagonist of that season in which he won the Grand Prix of San Marino at Imola and Zandvoort, Holland; it is highly probable that, if he had not been involved in that serious accident in the Grand Prix of Germany at Hockenheim during qualifying, which started in heavy rain, he would have taken the world crown at the end of the season. Below, centre: Patrick Tambay, who took Gilles Villeneuve's place, in the pits while the mechanics attend to the front of his 126 C2. Bottom, right: a close-up of the exhausts of the two KKK turbines fitted to the 6-cylinder 1500 cc engine of the Maranello single seater. The unit generated up to 580 hp at 11,000 rpm.

Left: the podium of the Grand Prix of San Marino at Imola. The race was deserted by the British teams for political reasons with the exception of Tyrrell, which permitted Michele Alboreto of Italy to take the first F1 podium placing of his career. Ahead of the future Ferrarista at the end of the race were the two Ferrari drivers, winner Didier Pironi and Gilles Villeneuve in second. The Frenchman beat his team mate by passing him on the last lap, contrary to his pit signals. The move attracted considerable criticism and is still the subject of discussion. A factor that would be the basis of the uneasy atmosphere at Ferrari during the transfer to the Zolder circuit in Belgium. The first inkling appears in this picture, which shows the dark, perturbed face of Gilles Villeneuve counterbalanced by the joy of Pironi for his victory. The two, who were great friends until that moment, did not talk out the incident in the days that followed and that weighed heavily on the tragic happenings in Belgium. A few months later, both drivers would still be missed by the Ferrari tifosi, as shown by the banner of the team's new standard bearer Patrick Tambay. It says, "Patrick, give us back Gil and Didi" and was exposed during practice for the Grand Prix of Italy at Monza.

1983 - 126 C3
The last title before the long wait

For 1983, Ferrari had engaged René Arnoux, who came to them from Renault, and, given the long-lasting convalescence of Didier Pironi, Patrick Tambay was also confirmed. The development of the optimum 126 C2 led to the C3 which, like its predecessor, was the best performer in F1. Tambay won at Imola before a crowd that had still not forgotten its idol Gilles Villeneuve and at least until mid-way through the season Ferrari's hopes were concentrated on him, while Arnoux had still not been able to achieve the results hoped for. But the simpatico new arrival René got into the fight for the world championship with a series of good placings, including wins in Canada and Germany.
A situation that translates into a possibility, slight though it was, of winning the title in South Africa, where drivers competed in the last Grand Prix of the year. The favourites were Nelson Piquet in his Brabham-BMW and Alain Prost in a Renault,

both powered by turbo engines like most of the cars in the world championship by then. But the place in the championship table was such that Arnoux hoped both of them would retire and that he would win the race so that his name would go down on the F1 role of honour. Unlikely, but not impossible. But the Frenchman was the first of the three to retire and his dream of bringing the title back to Maranello four years after Scheckter came to nothing.
However, the subsequent retirement of Prost enabled Ferrari to win the world constructors' championship yet again, even if it was unable to make the drivers' title its own. Arnoux was reconfirmed at the end of the season but Tambay was dropped in an unpleasant manner, leaving his place to a great hope of Italian motor racing, Michele Alboreto, the last driver to have been selected personally by Enzo Ferrari.

Patrick Tambay indicates to Alain Prost where to pass during the Grand Prix of Italy. At the start of the race, Patrick had the same number of points as Nelson Piquet, but the remaining results of the last 3 races were favourable to the Brazilian, who won the world championship. Meanwhile for Ferrari's Frenchman there was only a 4th place in the championship, "flavoured" with no renewal of his contract with Maranello for 1984. Right: the pits at Monza.

Above: in the two pictures on the left, a close-up of the simpatico René Arnoux and a moment in the pits with his 126 C3. Arnoux, who joined from Renault on the eve of the 1982 Grand Prix of Italy, and his win at Monza on that occasion partly mitigated the disappointment of the Ferrari tifosi, who were forced to console themselves 12 months later with a second and third place in the Italian GP by Tambay and Andretti. Arnoux, who in his youth was a mechanic for Conrero of Turin, disappointed in the first half of the season, having obtained only two podium places in seven races. With the Grand Prix of Canada he began a series of victories and second places, i ncluding the one at Monza, which put him back in the reckoning for the world championship, together with his team mate Tambay. But the arrival of no points at the penultimate race left the Frenchman with little hope of glory and he saw his world title chances go up in smoke with an engine breakdown in the early stages of the South African GP. The third picture above shows the monometer that controls the entry and exit temperatures of the air into and out of the turbine. Right: a close-up of Patrick Tambay, fired in unpleasant circumstances at the end of the season to make way for the promising Italian Michele Alboreto. Below: René Arnoux at Monte Carlo, a road circuit that did not bring palatable result to Ferrari this time either, a fourth place going to Tambay and a retirement for Arnoux after an accident on the sixth lap.

1999 - F399
First among the constructors again

For the first time in his career, Michael Schumacher was the victim of a serious accident that forced him into a number of weeks of inactivity. On 1 September he tried the Ferrari F399 during the usual testing session for the Grand Prix of Italy. The picture at the bottom, taken on that Wednesday, shows the German when he was convinced that there was a concrete possibility of soon returning to racing. When all said and done, the distance from Mika Hakkinen in the championship table meant there was still hope of catching the Finn. But the test produced a negative result and Schumacher decided not to compete in the Italian or German GPs. Mika Salo (above), another Finn, took his place and up until that moment had competed in four races in the F399 and in Germany abdicated from victory in favour of his team mate, Eddie Irvine.

Three seasons earlier, the leading post-Senna driver joined Ferrari: Michael Schumacher. In the previous 2 seasons, the German had lost the challenge for the title in the last race, but for 1999 the possibilities were firmer from the moment the F399 was the logical evolution of the cars that had preceded it. His team mate Eddie Irvine, in his fourth season with Ferrari, suddenly found himself in the role of candidate for the world title. On the first lap of the GP of Great Britain, a faulty braking system sent Schumacher crashing off the track and he broke a leg, so he had to miss a few races. That sent Irvine into orbit: with four victories to his credit, he went to the last race of the season at Suzuka, Japan, with a small but useful advantage over Hakkinen. For Eddie, it was fundamental to finish in front of his rival, but it was not to be. And the end of a season had numerous dark sides to it within the Italian team, with episodes that gave rise to many suppositions. Sudden technical deficiencies of the Ferrari being driven by the Irishman Irvine joined with a tragic-comic situation that that happened at the third last race, with the Ferrari idle in the pits for the usual stop, immobile on three wheels and with the mechanics desperately searching for the missing tyre. Result: 30 seconds lost and points that would have been useful. The subsequent Grand Prix of Malaysia had a mystery about it but ended up a 1-2 for Ferrari for the disqualification at verification because of lateral deflectors and the subsequent readmission after a few days, on the eve of the decisive race in Japan. Schumacher came back for the Grands Prix of Malaysia and Japan, but the German champion was only successful in his intention of bringing back the constructors' world championship to Maranello for the first time in 16 years. Ferrari won its ninth constructors' world title by four points from second placed McLaren-Mercedes, but that remained a partial disappointment due to the loss of the drivers', which slipped through their fingers for the third time when they were just a heartbeat away from success.

The mechanics with Michael Schumacher, who is in the F399 before taking to the track for one of the innumerable tests that the German has carried out in his long career at Ferrari. From his first day Schumy was able to motivate the whole team, including the men in the pits, with his commitment and ability. Mid-way through the 1996 season a series of breakdowns would have discouraged any driver. But Michael spurred on the work of the Ferrari men and results began to arrive. Not even the defeats of the following years, culminating with the error at Jerez in 1997 when he was fighting for the championship with Jacques Villeneuve, or at Suzuka in 1998 tarnished the high regard the team and tifosi had for him. The 1999 accident at Silverstone complicated matters, because for the third time in succession Ferrari had readied a car capable of winning the two world titles. Only Eddie Irvine, shown below at the chicane at the Monte Carlo harbour, was able to make a serious bid for the drivers' world championship after three seasons of appearance. Above, right: Irvine's first win. Next to him on the podium at the Grand Prix of Australia is Michael Schumacher's brother Ralf, who, it was said, was to have joined Ferrari. Things turned out much differently. Despite his results in the summer of 1999, Irvine was left free to find another team. The Irishman, an obedient servant of the team during his four seasons at Maranello, signed a big money contract with Jaguar.

2000 - F1 2000
A historic triumph

The winter that separated 1999 from the first year of the new millennium enabled Michael Schumacher to recover from the accident that happened a few months earlier, and the tifosi Ferrari's umpteenth disappointment with a title that was so near and yet so far away. The team of technicians, headed by Ross Brawn architect of the German driver's success at Benetton, further refined the car, increasing the power of the 10-cylinder and working on aerodynamic research, a basic element in modern Formula 1. The results were there as early as the first race in Australia, where the F1-2000 scored a 1-2 on its debut. It had already happened in the past that a brand new Rossa won on its first time out, like Eddie Irvine down under the year before. But it was back in 1979 in South Africa that Ferrari had scored a double during a first Grand Prix with all the opposition with it on the track. The memory suddenly became a good omen, but at the same time imperative because it was all those years ago that Ferrari last won both the drivers' and constructors' championships.
The most important new happening to Ferrari's status at the time concerned in the driver who replaced Irvine, who had moved on to Jaguar. Contrary to that which everybody thought, given his fine work during his three months at Maranello, it was not Mika Salo of Finland, but Brazilian Rubens Barrichello, a man with seven F1 seasons behind him but no victories. He was able to add his name to the list of drivers who had won for Ferrari at the Grand Prix of Germany at Hockenheim. For the pupil of the unforgettable Ayrton Senna, that was Barrichello's only victory of 2000, while the German champion won in Melbourne, at Interlagos and Imola. Then came two results in the points followed by another win in the three-race lead up to the Grand Prix of Monaco, all of which seemed to launch Michael towards an

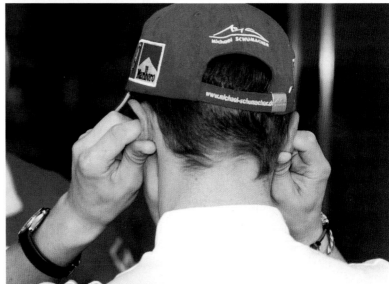

Two pictures of Michael Schumacher in his fifth season with Ferrari. Few drivers who preceded him stayed there that long. Up to then, only Jean Alesi, whose place the German took at the end of 1995, stayed that long. The lack of world titles in his first four years at Maranello caused some perplexity, but Michael did not listen and proceeded with his campaign for victory. The results proved him right, but it should not be forgotten that 2000 became a crucial time in his and the team's future, starting with a number of motor sport managers.

Left: Ferrari's new arrival, Rubens Barrichello. The Brazilian already had seven seasons of F1 under his belt and on his shoulders was the responsibility of continuing the tradition of the great champions from his country. Many, after the terrible loss of Ayrton Senna, pointed to Rubens as his successor. But that was not to be and, except for rare exceptions, Barrichello never gave the impression that he could excel. His arrival at Ferrari changed things a little, but the suspicion was confirmed that Schumacher did not have a great driver as his team mate. Below, left: two moments in a fundamental day in 2000. Michael on the grid of the Grand Prix of Italy talking with a technician about a final modification to his rear wing. Below, right: little more than an hour later, the joy of victory before the Italian spectators.

easy world championship. During the Monegasque race Michael retired with a technical problem, but then he won again in Canada with his rivals – especially Mika Hakkinen and David Coulthard of McLaren – seeming backward. Then Schumacher, who had changed the colour of his helmet in the meantime, retired from three consecutive Grands Prix due to first lap accidents in two of them, enabling his rivals to catch up. Especially Hakkinen, who won three races and took two seconds to top the drivers' championship table. The circus arrived at Monza for the Italian GP and Schumacher knew how important the race was to Ferrari's championship prospects, but also to the relationship that links his team with its home race. So after three previous failures he won. At the end of the race, his tears on live television were a sign that first the man then the driver were gripped by one of the most

emotional moments of his career and he had arrived at a cross roads. The next race had the flavour of a challenge about it, given that the event was at Indianapolis, homeland of American motor racing, which had returned to the F1 world championship after a 40 year absence. It did not happen on the classic oval of the historic 500 Miles, but the name was important and Ferrari celebrated its third 1-2 of the year there. So Maranello was able to travel to a Japan of bad memories with greater peace of mind than during the two previous years. And it was there, at Suzuka, that Schumacher satisfied an obsession that had lasted more than 20 years, winning the drivers' title at the wheel of a Rossa. Another two weeks and the constructors championship also became Ferrari's, marking the year with yet another similitude with 1979, the last previous year of the company's double.

Above, right and opposite: two pictures of Rubens Barrichello in the F1 2000. The driver from San Paolo debuted well in the Grand Prix of Australia, following his team mate like a shadow both in qualifying and the race. His year was one of sporadic results up until the race of his life, the Grand Prix of Germany at Hockenheim.

To a day of changeable weather was added the invasion of the track by a spectator that complicated the situation. But that day, as would be the case on others, Rubens was simply superlative and deservedly won his first F1 World Championship race. Below: an embrace between Jean Todt and Luca Cordero di

Montezemolo, the two men fundamental to the long history of the Prancing Horse. Montezemolo, who had already been the Scuderia's's motor sport director in the Seventies during the time of Niki Lauda's triumphs, and Clay Regazzoni, returned to Maranello in 1991 as president of the company, sent by major shareholder Fiat.

They were difficult years and he was the first to say the road to success would be long and hard. Two years later, Todt arrived at Ferrari in time for the Grand Prix of France, a man who had previously contributed in a different way to Peugeot's world championship rally, cross-country marathon and sports car racing successes.

2001 - F2001
Michael does it again

Having brought the drivers' title back to Maranello after 20 years did not satisfy Ferrari which, with the new F2001 repeated the previous year's success with an even more crushing defeat of its rivals. Michael Schumacher immediately made it clear that the number 1 on the nose of his car was well positioned by winning the first two races of the season in Australia and Malaysia. The opposition had been warned, which did not do much good because in the subsequent nine races he may not have won but he did come second with the exception of a retirement due to a mechanical breakdown at Imola. No rival could match him, so there was nothing to do but await the mathematical confirmation that the title belonged to the 30 year-old from Kerpen, Germany, again. His coronation could have taken place at Monza, but first there was a spectacular accident at the start in which he was involved, then after the re-start, fuel feed problems meant the celebrations had to be postponed. Three weeks later in Hungary, Michael won for the seventh time in 13 Grands Prix and the title was his with team mate

Rubens Barrichello right behind him for the third time. Ferrari also won the constructors' championship that day. The German was not happy with that, so he celebrated his title again at Spa, the track closest to his home town, by winning his fifth Grand Prix of Belgium, to which could be added that of 1994, which was taken from him after post race verification.

Monza was waiting to welcome the two Ferraristi to continue the celebrations, when the world tragedy of 9/11 also touched the golden world of Formula 1 in various ways. The atmosphere seemed unreal and it was the Ferrari number one who tried to convince his colleagues to stage a demonstration at the start of the race. The German only came fourth, a result many saw as the driver's means of not having to stand on the podium. The tifosis'"party" was postponed until the following month at the now well-established Ferrari Day, which was to be at Monza anyway. The season closed with success at the last race at Suzuka, which brought Ferrari's victories in the Formula 1 World Championship to 53, a record.

Above, left: Rubens Barrichello in the F2001 that could have brought him the joy of victory, but for various reasons in this world championship it still enabled him to climb onto the podium 10 times, but without winning. Above, right: Michael Schumacher, having retired mid-race, congratulates his brother Ralf, who had just won the Grand Prix of San Marino in his Williams. Right: the two F2001s at Monza without any sponsors' logos to mourn the victims of the terrorist attack on 11 September, the eve of the race. The world was confused at the time and the F1 circus was worried about its imminent race at Indianapolis.

Above: Michael Schumacher on the narrow roads of Monte Carlo in a race he won for the fifth time, the third in a Ferrari, with Barrichello second. When Michael scored his first win for Ferrari in the 310 B in 1997 Barrichello came second, but on that occasion the Brazilian drove a Stewart SF1- Ford and was followed in third place by Schumacher's team mate Eddie Irvine. Below: the two drivers of 2001 in their "offices". The cockpits of modern single seaters are the size of the driver and to leave them it is necessary to detach the steering wheel, as Barrichello is doing.

2002 - F2002
There is nothing for anyone

Ferrari continued to dominate Formula 1 in 2002, a season that would take people's memories and statistics back to 50 years earlier and the triumphs of Alberto Ascari in the 500 F2. While it was ready in the winter of 2001, Maranello's new weapon, the F2002, was not raced until the third Grand Prix in Brazil, where Michael Schumacher won after his victory in Australia and third in Malaysia, a race won by his brother Ralf in a Williams-BMW. It seemed that the younger Schumacher and his team mate Juan Pablo Montoya could have been a threat in the Ferrarista's new charge towards the world title. But the reigning world champion won the next three Grands Prix and that was enough to dash any hope of success by his rivals. At Monaco, his second place on the heels of winner David Coulthard in a McLaren was just a little

contention for the others, given that from then on Ferrari did not make a wrong move and won every race, including seven 1-2s. In the Grand Prix of Austria at Zeltweg just before Monte Carlo Barrichello had a real chance of winning the second F1 race of his career, but team orders took that much-deserved possibility from him. However, 23 June was his day in Germany again as with two years earlier; he won the Grand Prix of Europe at the Nürburgring ahead of his team mate, who was told not to attack the Brazilian in the closing stages of the event. A month later in France, Schumacher won the race and the world championship due to a mistake by McLaren's Kimi Raikkonen, who was on his way to his first F1 win. On that 21 July the Ferrari clan celebrated at the end of the day with

their president Montezemolo, who arrived on a direct flight from Maranello. The only person missing was Barrichello, who was disappointed with his car because it broke down at the start of the warm-up lap, taking him out of the race even before it started. But at the end of the season, he came second in the world championship table and ended up with four Grand Prix wins to his credit.

Michael Schumacher, above left, gets out of his F2002 that took him to the podium in every race of the season. Above, centre: Luca Badoer and (right) Luciano Burti, Ferrari test drivers. For many years, Badoer was the hidden architect of the successes of the team's drivers and could have taken Schumacher's place after his accident at Silverstone in 1999. That season, the driver from Veneto, Italy, raced for Minardi but Ferrari preferred Mika Salo of Finland, who was under contract to BAR at the time.

Above: the arrival of the Ferrari duo at the Grand Prix of Italy at Monza, always stronghold of the world championship year. The two drivers had already dominated in Italy at Imola on 14 April with victory by Schumacher with Barrichello second in the San Marino GP. Five months later, the boot was on the other foot with Barrichello winning his third race of the season against the German's 10. The Indianapolis race ended the same way, but it was a sort of prank. Just before the finish, Schumacher slowed so that the two crossed the line together. The computer ruled that Rubens had crossed the line a thousandth of a second before his team's number one and victory was, quite rightly, his. That partially repaid him for the dishonour to which he was subjected in Austria, when Jean Todt (below right, talking to the Brazilian) ordered him by radio to let Michael pass after having literally dominated the race. The order caused considerable indignation among the spectators as well as the millions of enthusiasts throughout the world, but the team said the final result came before anything else. A result Rubens could clearly have achieved if one considers that the world constructors' championship arrived at Magny Cours, where the end-of-race photograph with Montezemolo (below left) was taken. After the French GP there were still six races to go with 96 points up for grabs, four more than second placed Williams-BMW had scored after all 17 of the season's races.

2003 - F2003-GA
In the name of Gianni Agnelli

Top: the two Ferraris racing at Imola in the fourth round of the F1 World Championship, where the Scuderia fielded the F2002 for the last time, but it was no longer able to stand up against the opposition. In fact, only the home race brought Ferrari victory as well as the first podium finish of the season for the reigning world champion Michael Schumacher.

The team's new weapon made its debut at the next Grand Prix in Spain: the F2003-GA. At the presentation of the new car the initials GA were added to the usual designation of the car to honour the memory of the late head of Fiat, Gianni Agnelli, who died at the beginning of the year. Above: one of Agnelli's many visits to Ferrari during a test session.

Grand Prix of Australia, opening race of the 2003 season: the F2002 did not put its driver on the podium because Michael Schumacher only came fourth. Subsequent rounds in the Formula 1 World Championship created apprehension at Maranello, so Ferrari decided to field its latest creation: the F2003-GA. The name followed a simple practice by adding the initials of the Fiat number one, Gianni Agnelli, who died at the beginning of the year. After an uncertain start, the German and his new single seater confirmed their superiority and won four Grands Prix out of five at the beginning of the European season. Unlike previous years, though, the competition did not limit itself to containing the damage but counterattacked, creating other rivals: Kimi Raikkonen of Finland and Juan Pablo Montoya of Columbia, who disputed the championship with the Ferrarista. In the meantime, Schumacher's team mate Rubens Barrichello won a Grand Prix at Silverstone, marked by an invasion of the track by a spectator, as happened to him in Germany three years earlier. The season was also one of a psychological and legal battle between the tyre suppliers, those of Ferrari different from the tyres of its adversaries: a factor that created severe controversy at the start of the Monza race by Schumacher, who had not won for the last five races. With the European season at an end, there remained just the Indianapolis and Suzuka Grands Prix. In the States, Michael was superlative and won, but everything was put off until the last race, where he competed with excessive nervousness and was only able to come eighth, but that was still enough to give him his sixth world crown, a record, which also made Maranello the world champion constructor again for the fifth time in succession and 13 overall. Another record.

Rory Byrne, left, the talented South African designer who, together with Ross Brawn as technical director, enabled Benetton to win three drivers' and constructors' F1 World Championships in the mid-Nineties. After a break, in 1997 Byrne was engaged by Ferrari, which had put Brawn under contract in the meantime, as well as the triumphant Schumacher, to bring together a trio that was already a winner. In a short while, they also took the Rossa to the top. Among the new developments from the Ferrari technicians this season were the drums in the photograph top right, which enabled the team to definitively seal the brake block with the appropriate air intake. That was one of the many technological introductions that testify to a high degree of research Formula 1 had reached. Centre: a moved Michael Schumacher received the honours for having won the Grand Prix of San Marino. But the heart of the great German champion was broken by the death of his sick mother, which happened in the early hours. Despite that situation, the Ferrari driver and his brother Ralf, who drove for Williams, decided to face the sad and emotional situation, asking only - and quite rightly - to be left free of all commitments that were not strictly linked to their profession as drivers. The black armband on Michael's right arm testifies to that particular moment.

2004 - F2004
Record after record

A look at the sky by Michael Schumacher. At the end of the season, the German champion further increased his record collection of world titles, making all the star drivers before and after him to look up to him.

Having won the title in the last race of 2003, Ferrari realised that they could not drop their guard because their adversaries would not give in and include top names of the calibre of Honda, Renault, BMW, Mercedes-Benz, Toyota and Ford directly involved in Formula 1 either with their own teams or as engine suppliers. No time to take it easy, so the Scuderia went into battle with a car that was all but unbeatable: the F2004. As with their five previous creations, the newborn car won on its first appearance, a sign of hope. Nothing new, one might say. But there was a difference which, compared to its predecessors, was the consistency shown by the F2004, which could not find any adversary able to stand up to is in the subsequent four races. Only an accident at the chicane at Monte Carlo harbour momentarily the dictatorship of the umpteenth Brawn-Byrne car, which came into its own again at the next Grand Prix at the Nürburgring and continued to win for another six races from the Canadian GP to the Hungarian, scene of the seventh 1-2 of the year with the ever-present Rubens Barrichello. The following Grand Prix of Belgium also saw Schumacher and his team mate cross the finish line in that order, but for the second time that season Ferrari did not win the race on the day that Michael's F1 World Championship for drivers' score went up to seven. The constructors' title became Maranello's in Hungary on 15 August: a simpler formality than that for the drivers. The superiority of the F2004 was so manifest that the Ferraristi were able to decide to start at Monza with intermediate tyres and then stop after a few laps. After they re-started, they rejoined the race last but climbed their way back up the field to finish once again in a 1-2 parade, which earned them the usual invasion of the track by their adoring tifosi.

This time, though, the orders were the other way around,

After the negative experience of the previous season, with the early races lost despite having the best car, Ferrari decided to run the new F2004 right from the opening Grand Prix of Australia. That decision was repaid with five victories in the first five races of the season, including three 1-2 finishes that left little hope for even the best of the opposition. Among the drivers who began to make themselves known was Spaniard Fernando Alonso. To some, the Renault driver had taken the place of Michael Schumacher as the 'pupil' of Flavio Briatore, the Italian manager who did so much for the German in his victorious early years in Formula 1. Right: a moment in the duel between the two drivers, which started in 2003, the season in which Alonso became a top driver. It would be the Asturian who would take Michael's place as world champion during the following two years, narrowly beating the Scuderia's star in 2006. After his two brilliant years at Renault, Alonso was often approached by Ferrari, and, especially during the stormy 2007 at McLaren his move to Ferrari seemed certain. Instead, the title was won by Raikkonen and that postponed Fernando's arrival in Italy.

with Barrichello winning his eighth race in five years against 47 of his "number two" team mate. The subsequent Grand Prix of China, an absolute first for Formula 1, went to the driver from San Paulo, a result followed by pole position and the lowest step on the podium in the last race of the season on his home circuit in Brazil. An affirmation which is not metaphoric in Barrichello's case as he was born in one of the houses that surround the track.

With the conquest of the constructors' and drivers world championships, Ferrari's fifth in succession, the Scuderia peaked in this golden period and in the two seasons that followed, the two titles of 2006 slipped through the team's fingers – but only at the end of the last race of the year -, even though their multi-world champion from Germany won another eight races. On the one hand a laxity of logic that many observes had been expecting for some time, on the other a sudden change of the

regulations starting in 2005 demanded tyres that had to last for the entire length of a Grand Prix. Except for the following year, in which the change was reintroduced for the duration of testing and the race. Considering the difference of the Ferrari supplier and the key adversaries, this point represented a fundamental gap in the battle with the Scuderia's rivals, as shown in 2005, when the team only won at Indianapolis, undoubtedly facilitated by the retirement of seven of the 10 teams competing for the world championship as a technical choice connected to safety. Among the opposition there was the rise once more of McLaren-Mercedes-Benz, the last team to have defeated Ferrari in the by then distant previous decade, but the world titles went to another constructor – Renault who with Spaniard Fernando Alonso won the championships during the last two seasons in the Formula 1 career of Michael Schumacher.

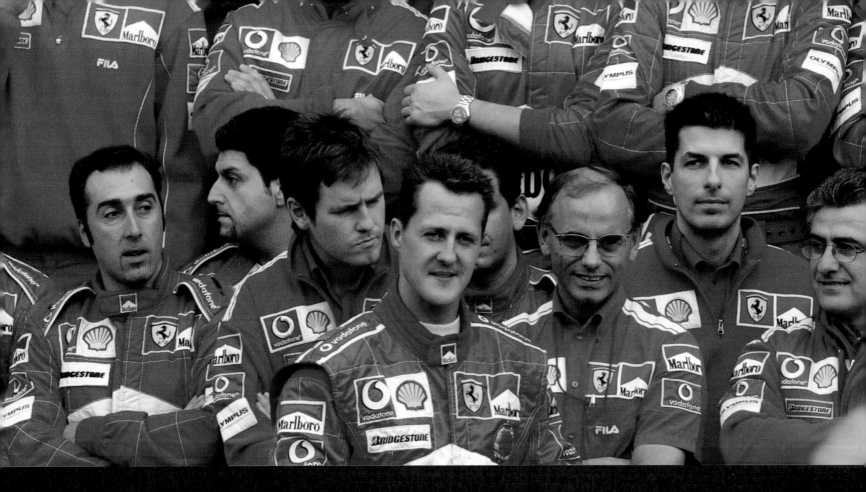

Opposite and above: two pictures showing Michael Schumacher together with the Ferrari mechanics. Although without particular demonstrations in public, the German champion has always considered team work fundamental, including that of the mechanics, often wrongly thought of as simple executors of some-

one else's orders. Below, left: at the annual Ferrari Day at the end of the season the six cars that had brought Ferrari 11 world drivers' and constructors' titles were fielded. The picture is, rightly, a celebratory moment that certainly cannot make predict that the Italian team would not be able to reconfirm its strength.

Especially the following year, when the only race won by the Scuderia would be the Grand Prix of Indianapolis, deserted by its rivals on the starting grid. Rubens Barrichello left Ferrari at the end of 2005 after six years as a faithful executor of the team's directives. He was only able to show his true ability on a few occa-

sions, sometimes turning out to be better than his outstanding team mate. Below, right: a symbolic photograph that accompanied the Italian constructor at all the world's circuits at which it appeared, as a testament to a unique and irreplaceable marque in the history of motor racing.

Schumacher: from champion to legend

Before Michael Schumacher there were five, six, not many more greats who associated their names with that of Ferrari. After the German, there may be one or two – or perhaps nobody at all – to whose name you can add the word unbeatable. Eleven years with the Rosso, not one of them without at least one victory and 11 world championships in total between his personal titles and those of the team. A result few, if anyone, will be able to aspire, perhaps for decades to come. A few who fly in the rarefied air reserved only for Grand Prix hunters first and titles second. When he arrived at Maranello, the man from Kerpen, Germany, was already basking in glory, with two world championships to his credit despite the tragedy at Imola that cost Ayrton Senna his life, depriving Michael of an adversary of his level. But at that time one could have imagined that in a hypothetical future the 10 years' difference between them would, anyway, have weighed increasingly in favour of the European. Schumacher became a "post-Senna"

driver, but what he showed in 16 seasons cannot be limited to the beginning, to the Benetton titles with the priming from Flavio Briatore. He shone right from his debut with Jordan and in the subsequent early approaches towards the podium, inflexible in his battles with his rivals who, apart from the great Ayrton, are Piquet, Prost and Mansell. Fearsome names.

Two titles, changing engine supplier from one year to the other but not his team, and then his arrival at Ferrari for the start of another adventure at the end of 1995, to do again that which an unknown Niki Lauda achieved 20 years earlier: cancel out the years of defeat. The first attempt was not a success, but all things considered that was not what he was asked to do. It was to reform the team and he was one of the right men for the job. The other, Eddie Irvine, a little less so, but that was really a help to the German. As early as his second year at Ferrari in 1997 he was on the right road to make people forget Jody Scheckter and

Various moments in the career of Michael Schumacher during his golden years at Ferrari. From the exacting entry into a chicane on the opposite page to the decisive look that shows a unique analytical ability. Among the habits of the German driver when he won was his traditional leap in the air on the podium – as well as an explosion of joy inside him – which demonstrated his tremendous stamina and physical ability in spite of the effort he had just put in to winning a race. Left: Schumy with one of his great loves, the motorcycle. Having ended his career he chose to compete on two wheels in Superbike, something unique rather than rare.

that long ago world title of 1979. But at the last race, Schumacher lost the tussle with Jacques Villeneuve in an unbecoming, dirty way and time was needed, victories too, so that people could forget the manoeuvre at Jerez in which he attempted to kick his adversary off the track.

The year afterwards it is still the Scheckter nightmare in his defeat by Finland's Mika Hakkinen. He continued with determination in 1999, but the leg he broke in the accident at Silverstone seemed to want to impede the Schumacher-Ferrari duo from rewriting history. A duo which, on paper, could become historic if everything went right. In 2000 things did go right and at that point the others could do nothing about it. He changed his team mate from Irvine to Barrichello, but it seemed more a formality, a statistic, punctuation. What remained was his persistent pursuit of victory, race by race, point for point, anything provided it was more than his adversaries. It did not matter if the figures showed he had double the

others' tally in the end, like in 2002, or only two more as in the subsequent championship. It was important that those years would be his, even after distant decades. Even in defeat, as in the case of his very last race. Brazil 2006, with the world title going to the Renault of his ex-mentor Briatore who, perhaps rightly, saw Michael's heir in Spaniard Fernando Alonso. Watching the German race, people asked themselves why a driver of his great talent was made to give up racing. In that Grand Prix, which we shall remember as the last of the Schumacher era, the German ended his career on the track with honour. He remained associated with the team that had given him so much, but which he had returned with so many victories and a new philosophy with that professional approach which, perhaps, those who preceded him at Ferrari did not have. Certainly, Schumacher raised the bar on what is considered the best, unattainable for almost all the drivers who have taken to the track since Brazil 2006.

2007 - F2007
The shadow of the 'spy story' over the championship

All Ferrari's men in the 2000s were replaced one by one. From drivers Michael Schumacher and Rubens Barrichello, the latter by his fellow countryman Filipe Massa, to technicians Ross Brawn and Rory Byrne right up to the head of the racing department, Jean Todt, who increasingly eased his grip on Maranello. Luca Montezemolo remained at

the top and, in the meantime, became Fiat's number one. For the new season Ferrari fielded the F2007 powered, as required by the regulations, by an 8-cylinder 2,400 cc engine and could no longer be the only team supplied with Bridgestone tyres. The company became the sport's single supplier from 2007.

But the year began under positive auspices with the classic opener in Australia that saw the winning debut in a Ferrari of its new acquisition from its adversary McLaren, Kimi Raikkonen. Historically, the battle between the two teams took place where it should unfold, on the track, even if in most cases since the mid-Seventies it emerged from the circuits to enter into those more cramped confines of a sports tribunal. In that sense, 2007 was a dark year, with the Anglo-German team implicated in an industrial spy story in which the principally damaged party was Ferrari. The result was a long series of decisions, sometimes controversial, first taken and then revised, which in the end produced a world championship riddled with suspicion. On the track, McLaren won the constructors' title with the sum total of points scored by its two drivers, reigning world champion Fernando Alonso and new star Lewis Hamilton, with 14 more than the Italian company. But a sentence passed by the International Federation during the season officially excluded Ron Dennis's team from the constructors' classification, consigning the title to Ferrari. The drivers' was in the balance right up until the last cut and thrust race in San Paolo and the internal fight between the now discharged Alonso and the team mate he did not much like – Hamilton – favoured Raikkonen who, helped by Massa's second place, won the title in his first year with Ferrari.

Ross Brawn and Nigel Stepney, two technicians who left Ferrari in a short space of time. While Brawn was attributed all the honours and recognition for his work, for Stepney there would actually be magistrates' charges for not-very-professional operations, an integral part of the famous spy story destined to rattle the very heights of McLaren, the implicated team together with Stepney, guilty of having consigned delicate information to them. After months of investigation and negotiations at all levels, an agreement was reached between the two teams, even if the summer of 2007 will remain one of the darkest periods in the decades-long history of Formula 1.

Above, left: the nose of the Rossa carrying the new Fiat logo. For 30 years, the Turin group, owners of Ferrari since 1969, has appeared in an official manner on the cars of Maranello to testify to their union. Ironically, Alfa Romeo and Maserati, two historic Italian marques that were also the rivals of Ferrari's rivals and its founder, eventually became the property of the Fiat group. Centre: the podium of the Grand Prix of Australia with Ferrarista Kimi Raikkonen in the middle after his winning debut with the team. With him is Jean Todt making one of his last appearances at the helm of the Scuderia, and the two McLaren drivers Fernando Alonso and Lewis Hamilton. The Melbourne race was the first of the year and these three drivers could not imagine that they would all be in the running for the world title at the season's last race in Brazil seven months later. There were another 15 Grands Prix to go as well as the spy story, which would be one of the determinate elements of the electric situation at McLaren, all to the advantage of Ferrari. Before the circus moved outside Europe at the end of the season, the team decided to put its money on Raikkonen instead of Felipe Massa. The driver from San Paolo put a decisive stop to his title chances with his retirement from the Grand Prix of Italy at the first corner (top right) so he put himself at the disposal of his team mate for the remaining four races.

2008 - 248 F1
A world title at the last corner

During the winter of 2008 the spy story of the previous season was still in the air, with recourse to the law. Then, as the year wore on, Ferrari and McLaren found grounds for agreement that would bring the matter to a close. But on the track the two rightly continued to fight it out as they had for 40 years with alternating fortunes. The same was the case in 2008, but this time the silver car overtook Kimi Raikkonen's and Felipe Massa's 248 F1, the drivers having been reconfirmed by the Scuderia but with the possibility of being able to back the best placed man and without obeying the pre-established order, considering that after all there was a reigning world champion in the team. After five Grands Prix, the two Ferrari stars had two victories a head and it would only be the subsequent mid-season events that would tip the scales as far as Massa was concerned.

The Brazilian had matured, but as had already happened in the past to Eddie Irvine in the key moment of the season he was let down by the team, which cost him two probable victories in Hungary and at the new night race at Singapore. The former for an engine breakdown and the latter in Asia just a few kilometres from the end due to a tragic-comic mistake when refuelling. But the situation remained open until the last race in San Paolo, where Ferrari had everything to gain and everything to lose. The weather at the Intelagos race wreaked havoc at the start and only on the last lap was each driver's strategy clear after the fourth placed driver, Britain's Lewis Hamilton in the McLaren, had crossed the line was there any certainty that Formula 1 had its first coloured world champion and also the first to win the drivers' title. Massa won the race like the star he was before his home crowd, but with tears in his eyes he could only console himself with having been the architect with Raikkonen of Ferrari's 16th world constructors' title in the legendary history of the famous Scuderia.

The reigning world champion Kimi Raikkonen besieged by the television cameras of the various channels. The Finn disappointed during the season, alternating good performances with bad. A year after his triumph at Interlagos, he would have to place himself at the disposal of the team to help his colleague Felipe Massa, on the right in the F2008 at Monza, in the Brazilian's attempt on the championship.

Above: Kimi Raikkonen's Ferrari leaves the pits with the number 1 on its nose. In this period the numbering of Maranello's cars varied little, mainly during the Michael Schumacher era. Below, left: after ending his driving career, the German champion was still available to Ferrari as a super-consultant but without obliging him to attend races. Nevertheless he worked from the pits on some occasions, giving the team the benefit of his advice. In addition, far from the prying eyes of the press, he also tested the Scuderia's single seaters preferring, however, to concentrate his great abilities on the development of a number of road cars.

With the departure of Ross Brawn, Rory Byrne and Jean Todt plus other members of the internal organisation and management, Michael remained one of the few representatives of that great revolution by president Montezemolo in the mid-Nineties which, especially after the Stepney case, meant that some technicians had to get used to working in the pits as in the photograph on the right. The promotion of new people such as Stefano Domenicali to motor sport director, and the changeover of other members of the team was another switch in direction in the recent history of Ferrari.

The adversaries of the modern era

While Michael Schumacher was winning his second Formula 1 World Championship at Benetton, he was negotiating with Jean Todt and everything was finished, or better it started, with his arrival at Maranello at the end of 1995. He had to go back to winning because the championships of Brabham, Williams, McLaren and Benetton hurt. As had happened in the past, the Scuderia searched for the best available – a guarantee of good results – and the first two years confirmed the team was right in the choices it made, with the champion from Kerpen the protagonist, even if he was beaten by Damon Hill and Jacques Villeneuve in their Williamses. Both of Sir Frank's drivers clashed with Michael on the track and not just metaphorically, creating the kind of controversy that continues to the present day every time their names are mentioned. With the Williams domination at an end, up cropped the name of McLaren again with the support of an old rival, Mercedes-Benz. The German

had been back in Formula 1 for just a few years, but by this time they were ready to win and they did so twice on the trot mocking the Rosso from Maranello at the last race. In Japan once more, Mika Hakkinen punctured the hopes of Schumacher and Irvine and brought back the veiled smile of presumption to the boss of the British team, Ron Dennis. With Ayrton Senna gone, the ex-Brabham mechanic of the Sixties was left short of champions and victories. Mercedes and McLaren did it in the last two years of the last century even if they did pay for it by not winning another title for a decade until a young man raised in the company named Lewis Hamilton brought back to Britain the drivers' title.

During the 5 years of the Ferrari reign there were those who put themselves in the frame but with poor results. Like McLaren, Williams went to German and BMW to find itself some engines. It engaged the brother of the champion, Ralf Schumacher, but only with the tough Juan

Lewis Hamilton was the surprise of 2007. Opposite: the British driver was predestined for the career he had had at Ron Dennis's team before entering Formula 1. As well as his undoubted qualities the colour of his skin contributed in a fundamental manner to turn him into a personage. After coming close to winning the drivers' world championship in his first season in F1, he was able to actually win it the following year. Below: Michael Schumacher flanked by the two Williams drivers in 1996. On his right is Jacques Villeneuve, with whom the German would be a protagonist the following year of a fiery season. On his left is Damon Hill, another driver whom Michael literally clashed on more than one occasion when he was driving for Benetton.

Above: Mika Hakkinen in his McLaren. The Finn was said to have been all washed up after his serious accident in Adelaide in 1995, after which he was in a coma for many days. Yet afterwards, he was able to prove the sceptics wrong and come back to F1 stronger than even. In 1997, Hakkinen won his first world championship Grand Prix the day Jacques Villeneuve humiliated Schumacher. In the two subsequent years, it was Hakkinen who beat Ferrari – in the last race of the season once more. Centre: Juan Pablo Montoya. The Columbian made an impression for the effrontery with which he faced his rivals when he came to Formula 1. His seasons first in Williams and then at McLaren were not the success that critics expected after his first few races. Below: Fernando Alonso with Renault, which took over Benetton and one that would always be linked to some of Michael Schumacher's great victories.

Pablo Montoya was it able to dent Ferrari's armour plating a little. Once Hakkinen had retired, Finland provided McLaren with another talented driver in Kimi Raikkonen as the compatriot to compete in the last dash with Schumacher in Japan. He lost and, after years of sufferance, joined Ferrari to win the title that was one of the strangest in the history of Formula 1. The last driver to get in the way of the implacable German and successful in his intent was a Spaniard who went to the top with the support of Flavio Briatore. Fernando Alonso successfully claimed the titles for Renault before reaching agreement with McLaren, only to discover as the championship progressed that the British team was not his ideal environment. Having returned to Renault, he could only watch as the battle for the 2008 championship was fought out between his hated ex-team mate Lewis Hamilton and the consistent Felipe Massa, hoping that one day he would drive a Rossa as had many other champions.

World Sports Car Championship

What is a race? How does one live it?

"It is a clamorous episode that today is concluded in Formula 1 in two hours of fascinating spectacle. **You must not forget endurance races, like the 24 Hours of Le Mans, Daytona or Sebring, where representation mixes with a thousand unforeseen human and technical adventures.**"

Enzo Ferrari

Ferrari

1953
To the top immediately

Not many years after the institution of a world championship for drivers, the International Federation brought in another for marques. The first World Sports Car Championship was run in 1953, made up of seven races on three continents from Sebring in North America, to the Mille Miglia in Europe with the finale on the dusty roads of the Carrera Panamericana. Ferrari did not contest the American races and concentrated on the Mille Miglia, which took place at the end of April. Unfortunately, the works 340 and 250 MM did not cross the finish line at Brescia, where the winner was a privately entered 340 MM Vignale driven by Giannino Marzotto with his friend Marco Crosara. The Italian industrialist and his brother Paolo also took came fifth in the year's 24 Hours of Le Mans in the car; a race which is worth a season on its own if we consider that there were the factory cars of about 20 manufacturers among the categories. The new Ferrari 375 MM made its debut in the Sarthe marathon and as the season continued it won two subsequent world championship races, the 24 Hours of Spa and the 1,000 Kilometres of the Nürburgring. In early September, Ferrari decided not to compete in the Tourist Trophy, concentrating all its efforts on the Grand Prix of Italy. For that reason, perhaps, Aston Martin DB3s came first in the Northern Irish event driven by Peter Collins and Pat Griffith and second with Reg Parnell and Eric Thompson. Third was the Jaguar C Type of Stirling Moss and Peter Walker, which brightened Maranello's chances of winning the world title at the last championship event in Mexico. Ferrari sent its motor sport director Mino Amorotti to the Carrera to support Scuderia Guastalla, which acted as a semi-works team. With the fourth place of Fabrizio Serena di Lapigio and Guido Mancini in a Pinin Farina bodied 375, Ferrari scored enough points to become the first team to win the WSCC. At the same time, Enzo Ferrari was having discussions with Alberto Ascari and Gigi Villoresi for the renewal of their contracts and let the press to speak about his threatened possible retirement from competition. The negotiations with the two drivers failed but, fortunately, the proposed retirement of the Prancing Horsing from racing did not happen.

Having passed into history as the first Formula 1 world champion driver with Alfa Romeo, Nino Farina was a driver who had been associated with Enzo Ferrari since the Thirties. In the post war period he competed with various cars, especially Maserati, until he joined the Scuderia definitively at the start of 1952. He drove single seaters in particular, and only competed in covered wheel cars in six world title races. He is pictured above at the first of them, the 1953 Mille Miglia in which he drove a 340 MM.

Above: three of the 15 Ferraris with nine different bodies and engines at the Grand Prix of the Autodrome at Monza on 29 June, which did not count towards the world championship. In the front is Piero Scotti's 250 MM, followed by Argentinean Roberto Bonomi in a 250 S, while the driver hanging out of the cockpit of the 225 S is Antonio Stagnoli. By the end of both heats they had taken the eighth to tenth places in a race won by Luigi Villoresi in a works 250 MM. As well as victory at Monza, Gigi also won the Giro di Sicilia; the Scuderia also won other important races not valid for the world title, including the Coppa d'Oro delle Dolomiti and the 12 Hours of Pescara and of Casablanca. At the end of the season, the first World Sports Car Championship went to Maranello.

Top, right: the 340 Mexico with a Vignale body was also privately entered: it was driven in the famous marathon by a promising young Italian named Eugenio Castellotti, but he dropped out with clutch trouble when he was lying 14th. Below: the Vignale bodied Ferrari 340 MM of Giannino Marzotto and Marco Crosara, winners of the Mille Miglia on 26 April 1953. It was Count Giannino's second victory in the event after his first win in 1950 driving a 195 S bodied by Touring. The 1953 success in a car from Maranello was the first ever win by the Prancing Horse in the World Sports Car Championship, even if it was not a works car.

1954
Winners throughout the world

Despite regret at having to lose its top driver Alberto Ascari, 1954 began well for Ferrari with victory in the first counter towards the World Sports Car Championship. In Buenos Aires, Nino Farina and Umberto Maglioli won the city's 1,000 Kilometres race at the end of January, the season's first of six rounds in the title chase. The Italian crew drove a 375 MM, but as early as the 24 Hours of Le Mans the great protagonist was the new 375 Plus, which was driven to victory by Froilan Gonzalez and Maurice Trintignant. And at the wheel of the same car, it was Maglioli who triumphed in the Carrera Panamericana. But the race victory that gave Maranello most satisfaction was the Tourist Trophy, in which Ferrari had not previously competed. On 11 September at the 12 kilometre circuit of Dundrod the Rossa, campaigned by Mike Hawthorn and Trintignant, defeated all the Jaguars, Maseratis and Aston Martins. Lancias came second and third having purloined Alberto Ascari and Gigi Villoresi, who were forced to retire on that occasion. With the Northern Irish victory having beaten all their British and Italian rivals, reigning champions Ferrari won the world title mathematically to once again demonstrate their great design capability with a car that was less powerful but more agile, the 750 Monza. During the season, important points also came from the exploits of another model: the 500 Mondial which, driven by Vittorio Marzotto, brother of Giannino and Paulo, on the Italian roads of the Mille Miglia came second behind the great Ascari in a Lancia D 24. Enzo Ferrari was pleased with the result, even if he knew in his heart that things would be difficult in the months to come with the arrival of the Mercedes-Benz 300 SL, the German constructor having started to compete in F1 mid-year with such success. And, of course, Mercedes would win three of the four 1955 races it

contested, among them their famous victories in the Mille Miglia and the Targa Florio. But the horrific accident involving Levegh's 300 SLR made the German manufacturer decide to abandon Le Mans, which would very probably have been won by the cars from Stuttgart.

The mechanics push the Maurice Trintignant-Froilan Gonzalez 375 Plus to the start of the 24 Hours of Le Mans. The other two works cars, driven by Manzon-Rosier and Maglioli-Paolo Marzotto, would retire with mechanical problems.
As is known, in the second part of his life Enzo Ferrari did not appear at the race tracks. But it was different the Fifties, when he was often at the Grand Prix of Italy at Monza or as in the photograph (left) at the verification of the cars in Brescias's Piazza della Vittoria that were to compete in the Mille Miglia.

Above: Vittorio Marzotto about to cross the finish line at Brescia on 2 May to take second place in the 1955 Mille Miglia and also win the 2000 cc class. The lone Italian industrialist, pictured below right at the start of the race at the wheel of his 500 Mondial.

The car was built towards the end of 1953 and its engine was derived from the 4-cylinder 500 F2, which driven by Alberto Ascari to beat all comers in the 1952 and 1953 F1 world championships.

The Mondial name was given to the sports racers and road cars as a tribute to those world titles. Below, left: another Ferrari - a privately entered 250 MM - campaigned by the Mille Miglia's most successful driver Clemente Biondetti, with four victories in the race to his credit. This time, he came 4th and 2nd in the over 2,000 cc class, beaten in that category only by the race winner, the great Alberto Ascari and his Lancia D 24.

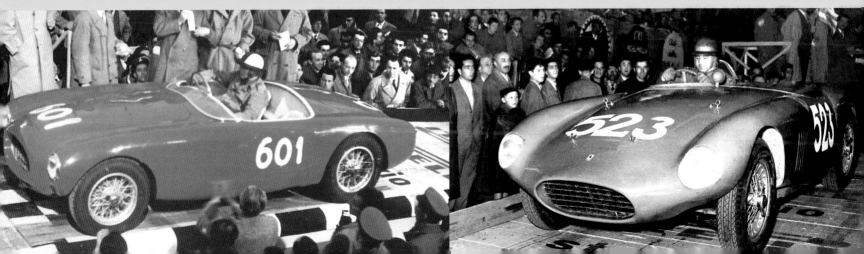

The rivals abound in sports car racing, too

World motor sport was reborn in the immediate post war period, with the Italian industry being able to succeed in its intention to excel better than others at a competitive level. Alfa Romeo and Maserati immediately snatched the top places, at least until they came up against a new marque that was officially born in the spring of 1947: Ferrari. The Modena constructor did not take long to become a point of reference on the European stage, and when in 1953 the International Federation instituted the World Sports Car Championship for endurance racing, Ferrari was there to accept the challenge that faced it from many different quarters. At the time, it battled with Alfa Romeo, which had left Formula 1

but was interested in sports car racing for commercial reasons, so much so that it entered the outstanding Juan Manuel Fangio for the 1953 Mille Miglia. The South American ace ended the season in another Italian works saloon, the Lancia D 24, in which he won the Carrera Panamericana. The Turin manufacturer would also be Ferrari's "bugbear" in 1954, winning a historic Mille Miglia with ex-Ferrarista Alberto Ascari before switching its attention to its Formula 1 single seater and leaving sports car racing. Another Italian team that battled against Ferrari starting in 1956 for two seasons was Maserati. The rivalry with the company that belonged to the Orsi brothers was sharpened by the logistical

The Mille Miglia of the Fifties was the race of the year. All the marques knew how important it was to prepare for this race in the best possible way as it was a sort of live advertising commercial for their products while it was being run. The Brescia-Rome-Brescia marathon had the right value, so all the great constructors came to the northern Italian city in an attempt to win. That was the case with Lancia on the opposite page, their D 24s at the centre of a massive crowd on verification day in 1954. They are the cars of Eugenio Castellotti, winner Alberto Ascari and Gino Valenzano. Top, left: another Ferrari rival, an Aston Martin at verification in 1953. The British constructor did not shine in the Mille Miglia, but it was able to win the 1957 and 1958 1,000 Kilometres of the Nürburgring. Bottom, left: Maserati at the start of the 1957 race with Stirling Moss. The British champion is shown above right at the start of the 1955 MM with the famous Mercedes-Benz 300 SLR number 722, in which he won in 1955.

closeness of the two marques, both Modenese. A fundamental role in that bitter rivalry was that of Fangio who, when he was asked to compete for one or the other, committed himself to the full, as shown, for example, at the 12 Hours of Sebring, which he won in 1956 for Ferrari and the following year for Maserati. The rivals of the Prancing Horse in that decade of world sports car racing were also to be found outside Italy's shores. Jaguar fielded its famous Type Cs and Ds, which beat the various Italian cars, but without ever winning as world title: one example in particular is the 24 Hours of Le Mans, which the British constructor won no fewer than five times in that decade. Then there was

Mercedes-Benz with its 300 SL in 1955 and, four years later, Aston Martin. While the Germans competed officially only in 1955 (with the ubiquitous Fangio in its ranks) with their crushing superiority, Aston Martin and the DBR1 made a hard job of beating Ferrari in 1959. At the end of the Fifties, another German car constructor appeared on the scene. It was Porsche, but it competed with cars of a lower cubic capacity compared to its Italian rivals; a factor that enabled it to especially excel in events over tortuous routes like the Targa Florio, while waiting to come out with a series of prototypes at the end of the Sixties that blew away all their competition, Ferrari included.

1956
Ferrari-Maserati: a world derby

For different reasons, the main adversaries of Ferrari left the World Sports Car Championship: Lancia and Mercedes-Benz. The 1956 season would be one of a challenge between the Prancing Horse and its hometown rival, Maserati. In this year's WSCC, which would only comprise five races, everything would be decided at the last event, the 1,000 Kilometres of Sweden on 12 August. Until that time, the results were equal with two victories apiece. Ferrari won its first 12 Hours of Sebring on 24 March thanks to new arrival Juan Manuel Fangio and local boy Eugenio Castellotti and, a month later, the prestigious Mille Miglia after a great drive by the young Italian. Before the American race, the two top Ferrari 410 Ss were forced to retire from the opening event in Buenos Aires with technical troubles. That is why the Scuderia chose the 860 Monza as its WSCC campaigner from then on. However, the Brescian win by Castellotti was the merit of the more powerful 290 MM. With the last round in Sweden on the cards, Ferrari

and Maserati, who were already battling it out between each other for the Formula 1 World Championship, prepared themselves in the best way they knew how and sent no fewer than five works cars each to the finale. Despite the retirement of the leading 860 Monza driven by Fangio and Castellotti after a handful of laps, the race was still a Ferrari success due to the victory of Phil Hill and Maurice Trintignant in their 290 MM, the resounding defeat of Maserati being completed by Peter Collins-Wolfgang von Trips second in a similar car and Alfonso de Portago-Mike Hawthorn-Duncan Hamilton and Peter Collins taking third in another 860 Monza. As well as the WSCC, Ferrari also won the Giro di Sicilia with new driver line-up Collins and Louis Klementaski, plus the Supercortemaggiore GP at Monza won by Collins and Hawthorn. There were two important classics that the Scuderia did not win that year, though, and they were the Targa Florio and Le Mans, won by Porsche and Jaguar.

Apart from the Ferrari works cars, others were often entered for WSCC races by private teams or private owners, like the one top left, a 250 Monza, which got back to Brescia after more than 15 hours of racing driven by its South American crew of Dos Santos-Araujo. The picture was taken, as suggested by the car's number, at 5.59 am and was followed up the starting ramp by Juan Manuel Fangio's 290 MM (right), the last driver to start.

Left: Luigi Musso's Ferrari 410 S in the opening race of the World Sports Car Championship, the 1,000 Kilometres of Buenos Aires. Third in qualifying, the driver from Rome and team mate Peter Collins had to retire soon after mid-way with a broken differential. The sister car driven by Fangio and Castellotti went out a couple of hours later with transmission woes. Below: Eugenio Castellotti about to cross the line at Brescia to win the Mille Miglia in a 290 MM on April 29, while his team mates Collins and Musso crossed the line after him to come second and third in the less powerful 860 Monzas. With the results achieved in the five rounds of the WSCC – two wins and one second place – Castellotti would certainly have been the world champion driver if such a title had been instituted in this special category.

1957
The last tragic Mille Miglia

In 1957 the battle for the World Sports Car Championship was between Ferrari and Maserati once again, with the latter immediately taking advantage of the divorce between Juan Manual Fangio and its Maranello rival by engaging the Argentinean. The world champion went back to having Stirling Moss as his team mate, as was the case two years

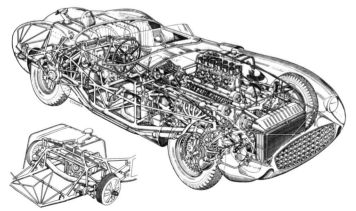

Above: the start of the Mille Miglia on 12 May and the long wheelbase Ferrari 250 GT of Luigi Gavazzoli, a gentleman driver who used the pseudonym Madero.

Below: a cut-away of the 250 Testa Rossa, a car that signalled an important change of direction for the Scuderia in motor sport.

earlier at Mercedes-Benz. It is curious to note that it was these two drivers who came first and second respectively in the 1956 F1 World Championship and would do so again in 1957, but were still adversaries in that Moss was at the wheel of the single seater Vanwall. Ferrari was putting his money on the Italian duo Eugenio Castellotti and Luigi Musso, both world stars by that time, animated by an internal rivalry, which was just how the Commendatore liked it. But in the spring, Castellotti lost his life in an accident at the Modena test circuit; it was the prelude to and even more horrific event two months later towards the end of the Mille Miglia in which Alfonso de Portago and Ed Nelson flew off the road a few kilometres from Brescia and killed themselves plus nine spectators. A tragedy that left its mark on Enzo Ferrari once more, but also on road racing itself. In that cursed race, the Italian constructor still triumphed with Piero Taruffi at the wheel of a works 315 S ahead of a sister car driven by Wolfgang von Trips; third was Olivier Gendebien of Belgium in a factory 250 GT. More than half the season had slipped by when Ferrari was roundly beaten at Le Mans, this time by Jaguar again, only managing to take fifth place with a 315 S driven by Britain's Stuart Lewis-Evans and the Scuderia's long-time test driver Martino Severi. Meanwhile Maserati, which did not finish at the Sarthe, won in Sweden and climbed up to within three points of Ferrari before the 1,000 Kilometres of Caracas. The race was a repeat of the previous year's situation with the two Italian constructors vying for the world championship in the concluding round. Ferrari was implacable on the roads of the Venezuelan capital, taking the first four places with its four works cars, none of its rivals ever seeing the chequered flag.

Above, left: Piero Taruffi's 315 S drives off the starting ramp on 12 May at the 24th Mille Miglia. At the time nobody had an inkling that, after 10 hours, the ageing Roman engineer would have triumphed in the Italian marathon. Even less so that the event would be the last in the series. Taruffi drove an intelligent race and his 315 S preceded its potent sister car across the finish line driven by Germany's Wolfgang von Trips. The feared rival Maserati 300 S with Giorgio Scarlatti at the wheel and the legendary mechanic Guerino Bertocchi crossed the line over 30 minutes later. Enzo Ferrari was especially pleased that, in front of the Maserati, was the less powerful Scaglietti-bodied 250 GT driven by Olivier Gendebien with Jacques Washer. Below: the Belgian crew crosses the finish line just eight minutes behind winner Taruffi, even though they were driving a much less powerful car. Above, centre: Alfonso de Portago drives his Ferrari 335 S down the Mille Miglia ramp to begin the race. The Spaniard, in a close-up on the right taken before the tragic race, was only a few dozen kilometres from the finish when his car left the road and killed a number of spectators as well as himself and co-driver, American Ed Nelson. The event was undoubtedly a major tragedy for Ferrari and the legal turmoil in which the Commendatore was involved for years. But he still won the race, his cars taking the first three places and class wins; in fact, 12 of his cars were among the first 16 home.

1958
Testa Rossa, act 1

During the 1957 season, a car destined to leave its indelible mark on the history of Ferrari made its debut almost incognito: it was the 250 TR. The two letters stand for Testa Rossa, a designation that would be taken up again in the Eighties by another successful road car. They were given that name because red was the colour of the cylinder heads of their 12-cylinder engines. The potential of the 1957 car exploded the following year when it totally dominated the World Sports Car Championship, won for the third time after 1953 and 1956 in the same year in which Ferrari made the F1 drivers' championship its own. To tell the truth, in this its first season the Testa Rossa had no direct adversaries in that Maserati, which had fought so hard against its eternal rival during the previous two seasons, did not compete officially. That left Porsche and Aston Martin, but they were not at most of the world championship races. The leading driver of 1958 in a Testa Rossa was Peter Collins, who won in Buenos Aires and at Sebring with his team mate Phil Hill. With his second place at the Nürburgring with his fellow countryman Mike Hawthorn, Peter brought the mathematical title to Ferrari. Unfortunately, exactly two months later the Briton lost his life when he went off the very same circuit during the Grand Prix of Germany. It was in that German 1,000 Kilometres that Ferrari suffered its first defeat of the season: an Aston Martin DBR1 came first, driven by Stirling Moss and rising star Australian Jack Brabham. It was the first warning of an adversary that also won the 1958 Tourist Trophy and the following year would fight with Maranello to the end to become the best marque in the world among the sports racing cars.

Above: the 250 GT Competizione, a car entered by Maranello for the Grand Touring races. Below, left: a close-up of Paul Frère and (right) another of Olivier Gendebien. The two Belgians were excellent Ferrari drivers and were the stars of many outstanding performances. Especially Gendebien, with 10 victories in world title counters of which no fewer than four were achieved in the 24 Hours of Le Mans. Another of his victories was in the 250 Testa Rossa at the 1958 Targa Florio. Opposite: Luigi Musso, who won the Targa Florio co-driven by Gendebien, in a 250 Testa Rossa.

1960
Yet another title at Le Mans

Ferrari only took third place in the last race of the 1959 season at Goodwood, where the winner was an Aston Martin DBR1, and virtually gave the WSCC to the British constructor, which did not compete in any of the five world title races the following year. It would have been easy at this point for the 250 Testa Rossa and its various works drivers Phil Hill, Cliff Allison, Richie Ginther, Wolfgang von Trips and others, to still win the title. But instead it was the little Porsche in versions 718, RSK and RS60 that complicated the plans of Enzo Ferrari by winning Sebring and the Targa Florio, while victory went to Maranello in the opening race at Buenos Aires on 31 January.

At the Nürburgring the win went to the resuscitated but unofficial Maserati driven by Stirling Moss and Dan Gurney, with the Allison-Willy Mairesse Ferrari third over a minute behind the smaller and more agile Porsche of Jo Bonnier and Olivier Gendebien. There remained only the most important race of the season, the 24 Hours of Le Mans. There were 13 Ferrari Testa Rossas and 250 GTs at the Sarthe event against a few Porsches, which were undoubtedly penalised by their smaller cubic capacity and lack of power on the long French straights. Of the four works Ferraris, the only one to finish was the one that mattered: the winning 250 TR driven by Paul Frère and Olivier Gendebien, who was in the cockpit of the German rival a few weeks earlier. Victory in France washed away the stain of the previous year, when not a single Ferrari finished the race. But the defeat suffered in the Italian round still hurt, Maranello having sent the higher performing 246 S to the Targa Florio; it was a car that also had the Testa Rossa's lines but was powered by a 2-litre engine instead of its bigger sister's 3000 cc.

Above: the Testa Rossa driven by Frenchman Jean Behra. The 1960 season was the model's fourth, but following a number of updates it would continue to compete until 1962.
Top: the Rodriguez brothers. Left: Ricardo, whose career came to an abrupt halt at 20 years-old in an accident in a Ferrari F1 car. The Mexican brothers competed in many endurance races in cars entered by American importer N.A.R.T., winning the 1,000 Kilometres of Paris a few days before Ricardo's accident. Despite the obvious human trauma, Pedro (top right) continued his career in sports racers, mainly driving a private Ferrari. In 1971, he was killed in a non-championship race driving a Ferrari Sport at Nuremberg.

Above, left: a picture of a 250 Testa Rossa winning the 1959 12 Hours of Sebring. At the wheel is ex-U-S. marine Dan Gurney, who alternated with Chuck Daigh. After the mid-race retirement of the Phil Hill-Olivier Gendebien Testa Rossa at the Florida circuit, the two drivers switched to this car, taking to four the names of the winners of the first round of that season.

Above, right: Gendebien at the 24 Hours of Le Mans in another Testa Rossa. He won again, sharing the triumph with fellow Belgian Paul Frère who, although entered for the 1960 Targa Florio in a Ferrari Dino 246 S, did not drive the car, which was taken to fourth place by Willy Mairesse, Ludovico Scarfiotti and Giulio Cabianca.

Below: Frère shown at the Sicilian event behind a policeman intent on readying his camera: when he retired from racing journalism would be his job until the last years of his life. The Ferrari in the picture is the 250 Testa Rossa of Wolfgang von Trips and Phil Hill, which came second. Note Pedro Rodriguez in the background (right) with his helmet in his hands waiting to take over the Dino 196 S being driven by his brother Ricardo. At the end, they would be third in class and seventh overall behind the agile Porsche 718 RS.

1961
From Sebring to Pescara, always at the top

The positioning of the engine from the front to the rear, but this time for the world of motor racing, also interested Ferrari.

In 1961, the Dino 246 SP was introduced with a 2,400 cubic capacity as indicated by its designation and would be a

Two cars, two masterpieces.
Above: the Dino 246 SP competing on the more than 70 kilometres of the 1961 Targa Florio route of 30 April. The car was originally assigned to von Trips-Ginther, but during the race motor sport director Romolo Tavoni decided to replace the American with Olivier Gendebien, who had retired after Phil Hill crashed their car.

After Gendebien's stint, the car was returned to the able hands of von Trips who, after a historic climb back up the field to catch Stirling Moss's Maserati, slipped into the lead to score Ferrari's second victory of the season in the championship. Below: the 250 Testa Rossa of Phil Hill and the ever-present Olivier Gendebien at Le Mans.

stablemate of the 156 that competed for the Formula 1 World Championship. The sports racer made its debut in the 12 Hours of Sebring, first race of the season, driven by Wolfgang von Trips and Richie Ginther but it retired. However, the Italian constructor won with the much more powerful 250 Testa Rossa (updated in its appearance and mechanics) crewed by Phil Hill and Olivier Gendebien. But it was at the wheel of the fast, agile Dino that the Belgian and von Trips won the year's Targa Florio, leaving the Maserati Tipo 63 of Nino Vaccarella and Maurice Trintignant to cross the finish line over half-an-hour later and second in the 3000 cc class. Ferrari's eternal rival raced again at the Nürburgring in the colours of the American team Camoradi and won the 1,000 Kilometres. On that occasion, the Tipo 61 was driven by Americans Masten Gregory and Lloyd Casner, while the works 246 SP of Ginther, von Trips and Gendebien, which came third, beaten by the private Testa Rossa of the young brothers Ricardo and Pedro Rodriguez. Ferrari also won the 24 Hours of Le Mans, its points decisive for the WSCC thanks to the Testa Rossa driven by Gendebien and Hill ahead of the sister car of Mike Parkes and Willy Mairesse. The only 246 SP in the event, driven by Ginther and von Trips, had to retire midway through the race. With the victory in the Sarthe classic and the 1961 World Sports Car Championship in his pocket, Enzo Ferrari decided to compete in the 4 Hours of Pescara with a 246 SP for Ginther-Giancarlo Baghetti and a Testa Rossa for Lorenzo Bandini-Giorgio Scarlatti, the latter entered by Mimmo Dei's Scuderia Centro Sud. And it was that car that won the Abruzzo race, in part due to the retirement of the only works Ferrari mid-way through the event with steering problems.

A picture that shows a moment in motor racing of the unforgettable Sixties. It is 15 August 1961 and the competitors in the 4 Hours of Pescara sprint towards their cars, lined up in front of the pits 24 Hours of Lea Mans start style. The dash from the other side of the track was typical of many endurance races, especially Le Mans, where it remained so until 1969. Then it was dropped from racing for logical safety reasons. Another thing this photograph suggests compared to today is that the start was not based on qualifying times but in the progressive entry number. The Abruzzo race, better known as the Coppa Acerbo, had a long history that began with Enzo Ferrari's victory in the first ever Coppa in 1924. Destiny meant that it was one of the Commendatore's cars that won the last race shown in the picture. The Maranello barchetta driven by the all-Italian crew of Lorenzo Bandini and Giorgio Scarlatti won the event: it was not a works car but one of Mimmo Dei's Scuderia Centro Sud. Ferrari wished to repay Dei for the help provided by the manager from Rome, who a few months earlier ensured a Cooper F1 car found its way to Maranello to enable the Ferrari technicians to better understand the secrets hidden away under the light body of the revolutionary British racer, which had dominated Formula 1 in 1960.

The Testa Rossa that won the 4 Hours of Pescara has a glorious yet tormented history. An accident scarred its debut in the 1960 Targa Florio with Cliff Allison. It won at the subsequent 24 Hours of Le Mans in the hands of Phil Hill-Olivier Gendebien. During the 1961 winter it was modified and was entered for Sebring, where it came second. It was involved in another accident at the Targa Florio, but it took second at the Nürburgring and Le Mans. Then it closed its extraordinary career on the French circuit by winning the 1962 event driven by P. Hill and Gendebien. By then it was no longer designated Testa Rossa but 330 TRI/LM.

1962
GTO: a Grand Tourer at the top of the world

In 1962, the International Federation introduced new World Sports Car Championship tables for covered wheel cars. As well as the prototype trophy it brought in the International Grand Touring Constructors' Championship, subdivided into various classes. Ferrari won the prototype with victories in all the races, which were the 12 Hours of Sebring, the Targa Florio and the 1,000 Kilometres of the Nürburgring with the 250 Testa Rossa in the United States and the Dino 246 SP in Sicily and Germany. As well as these triumphs, the Prancing Horse took the first three places in the summer's 24 Hours of Le Mans in its umpteenth display of strength.

In the GT series for cars of which a minimum of 50 examples had to be produced – at least on paper – Ferrari fielded the new 250 GTO, the designation standing for Gran Turismo Omologata. This two-door, even though driven by men under contract to Ferrari like F1 world champion Phil Hill and engineer and test driver Mike Parkes, was also raced by private teams and leading drivers like Britain's Graham Hill, Innes Ireland and John Surtees. The result was a season studded with splendid victories, culminating with victories at the 1,000 Kilometres of Montlhéry with four GTOs in the first five places and the success of brothers Pedro and Ricardo Rodriguez. The two youthful Mexicans were rising stars in the world of motor racing and Ferrari had a particular weakness for the younger of the two, Ricardo. The Commendatore provided the youngster with a Formula 1 car for the 1962 season, convinced of the young man's potential. Unfortunately, both of brothers would tragically lose their lives in the sport, but at different times. Although a negative year for the single seaters, the endurance season was a triumphant one for Ferrari and its undisputed leader, who had "decapitated" his staff a few months earlier and had to seek out new collaborators. In that break-up the star of Mauro Forghieri was born and he was a designer who would create some of the most famous and glorious Ferrari racing cars of all time.

Ferrari's cars for the 1962 season lined up in the courtyard of the legendary factory in Via Abetone, Maranello, for their presentation to the press. The Commendatore had for some time understood the importance of this moment, which was followed a few weeks later by an end of season press conference in which he discussed the year that was ending with journalists. Often on such occasions, Ferrari took the opportunity to give his own incontrovertible version of the facts, which sometimes did not correspond with the published stories. It was a way of winning a few special points concerning the job of journalism that he practiced, even if for a short time, when he was young.

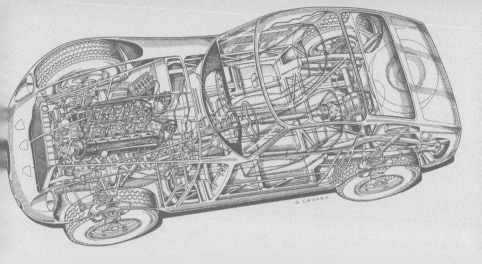

Above, left: a cutaway of the 250 GTO. Right: the car in a recent photograph. The sports saloon most famous and sought after by collectors in the history of Ferrari appeared in one of the Italian constructors most delicate moments. The idea matured in the summer of 1961 and its creators included Giotto Bizzarrini who, together with other leading lights at Ferrari like engineer Carlo Chiti and Motor sport director Romolo Tavoni, were fired during the autumn of that year. The development of the new car was carried out by the technicians that remained, among them the young Mauro Forghieri already stood out. Stirling Moss, a driver of whom Ferrari thought highly, was asked to test drive the car. The Briton, always a bitter rival of Ferrari's on the tracks of the world, spent whole days testing the car at Monza and Modena. That seemed the start of a collaboration which would bring the Briton to Ferrari, but in the spring of 1962 Moss was involved in a horrendous accident at Goodwood on Easter Day, which ended his career prematurely. Another great British driver marginally linked to the history of the Ferrari GTO was Graham Hill. Below: a pit stop during the 1963 Tourist Trophy, won by reigning world champion Hill in a car entered by Ferrari's British concessionaire. Hill and Moss had competed together in the 1961 24 Hours of Le Mans in a Ferrari 250 GT SWB and they were going well until they had to retire with cooling problems. While Stirling was forced to retire after the Goodwood accident, Hill continued to race Ferraris occasionally until 1965.

1963
Three titles in a year

Top: last act in a drama that lasted a thousand kilometres on the fearsome German Nürburgring for the John Surtees-Willy Mairesse Ferrari 250 P. The Belgian, who had been with the Scuderia since 1960, is smiling as he takes the chequered flag. He had a preference for endurance races, producing excellent results including a win in the 1963 Targa Florio. Ferrari had a soft spot for this man, who would have an accident at the next 24 Hours of Le Mans. The other 250 Ps did well in the French marathon, shown in the picture above. The winner was car 21 driven by Bandini and Scarfiotti, while a private 250 GTO came second, followed by another 250 P of Parkes-Maglioli.

For 1963, Ferrari went back to recruiting quite a number of Italian drivers for his team. Having lost Giancarlo Baghetti and ex-world champion Phil Hill, who moved to ATS, Ludovico Scarfiotti and Lorenzo Bandini where the men the Commendatore mainly put his money on, together with another from the world of motorcycle racing, seven times world champion John Surtees.

At the end of the year, Maranello began to see some light at the end of the Formula 1 tunnel in part due to the win of the Briton at the Nürburgring, while in the covered wheel car races Ferrari won three classes due to the excessive subdivision of the sport by the International Federation: they were the two classes of the International Prototype Trophy of up to and over 3,000 cc and the International Touring Car Constuctors' Championship, the most prestigious for over 2,000 cc cars. Having backed Italian drivers, two of them shot to the top with a first place by Bandini and Scarfiotti at Le Mans, which is still today the only victory in the world's most famous endurance race by an all-Italian crew. The triumph in France was achieved with the new 250 P, which was developed during the winter and was the first Ferrari to have a 12-cylinder engine installed in its rear. The car debuted in March by taking the first two places in the 12 Hours of Sebring with Surtees-Scarfiotti, then Willy Mairesse-Nino Vaccarella-Bandini, followed by another win at the 1,000 Kilometres of the Nürburgring with Mairesse-Surtees. The 250 GTO also scored the results hoped for, even if they were the merit of the usual teams linked to the company. It is from there that the victories of Pedro Rodriguez came in the 3 Hours of Daytona, Mairesse in the 500 Kilometres of Spa and the reigning F1 world champion Graham Hill in the Tourist Trophy at Goodwood.

Below: a Ferrari 250 LM unveiled at the Paris Motor Show in the autumn of 1963. The letters LM were a tribute to Le Mans and Ferrari's many victories there in those years, all of which was broadening the popularity of the Italian marque. It should not be forgotten that Ferrari was a step away from becoming an offshoot of America's Ford that summer, partly because of the "jealousy" of the interest this small constructor was generating in the world on a daily basis. The sports saloon had a 12-cylinder engine of over 3-litres, while the body had a roll bar that was an integral part of the engine cover. The car, designed by Pinin Farina, had great critical success but had trouble getting its sports homologation, which induced Enzo Ferrari into making a cla-morous protest a year later. He decided his single seaters would no longer compete in their traditional racing red in the last stages of their battle for the F1 world title and had them entered by his North American importer Luigi Chinetti painted in U.S. colours blue and white. Above, right: Enzo Ferrari shows his latest creation to Giorgio Gregori, at the time motoring correspondent of "Il Giorno". Above, left: a close-up of Ludovico Scarfiotti, an occasional Ferrari works driver for 10 years. His most famous F1 win was in the 1966 Grand Prix of Italy, but he also did well in sports racers, winning five world title events including the 1963 Le Mans. He was also a great mountain climber and was the 1962 and 1965 champion of Europe driving Ferraris.

1964
The Duel with the Americans begins

The John Surtees F1 World Championship in Ferrari's relaunch season joins those won for the third year in succession in the International Grand Touring Constructors' Championship. No fewer than 12 races made up the fixture list, with a special points scoring system joined the addition of events like hillclimbs and the Tour de France alongside the much more classical Targa Florio and the 24 Hours of Le Mans. The 250 GTO was, once again, the victorious car with an overpowering start to the season in the 2,000 Kilometres of Daytona, in which "homologated" cars took the first three places driven by winners Phil Hill-Pedro Rodriguez, then came David Piper-Lucien Bianchi, Bob Grossman-Walt Hansgen. Next up was Mike Parkes victory in a similar car in the 500 Kilometres of Spa plus prestigious placings; then there was the victory of the Belgians Bianchi-Berger in the penultimate counter, the Tour de France, which was run in September and that mathematically consigned the 1964 world title to the Scuderia. It was a season in which the main adversary was the AC Cobra, which had become a sort of sports emanation of Ford. In later months the Americans would challenge Ferrari on the track after the Commendatore's refusal to merge industrially with the car manufacturer when the small warrior of an Italian constructor was just a heartbeat from signing the contract in 1963. In the special prototype Trophy table, an absurd regulation deprived Ferrari of a meritorious win. The victory of the 275 P, a revision of the already high performing 250 P, with Parkes and Maglioli at the 12 Hours of Sebring, of Ludovico Scarfiotti and Nino Vaccarella in the 1,000 Kilometres of the Nürburgring and the Sicilian with Frenchman Jean Guichet at Le Mans were insufficient. As Ferrari did not compete in the remaining Targa Florio championship round, the Federation assigned the trophy to Porsche, which was the German constructor's first title in the long series.

Top: the private 250 GTO of Sweden's Ulf Norinder and Picko Troberg came ninth overall in the Targa Florio. The seven Maranello sports saloons were the only ones in the GT 3.0 class and the two Scandinavians came second in the category behind Italians Luigi Taramazzo and Corrado Ferlaino, who later became famous as president of the Naples FC in the days of superstar Diego Maradona. Below: the 275 P of Nino Vaccarella and Umberto Maglioli, who is driving, winning the 1964 12 Hours of Sebring on the first day of spring. This was an outstanding success for Ferrari, whose drivers occupied the entire podium and beat its new and anxiously awaited rivals, the Shelby Cobras.

Below: Umberto Maglioli in the early stages of the 1964 24 Hours of Le Mans, which started as usual on the Saturday afternoon. In the past, the Piedmontese was a works driver during the first three years of the World Sports Car Championship and was recalled in 1963 just for the French endurance race. He and Briton Mike Parkes came third the year afterwards and, as well as the victory in the 12 Hours of Sebring he was once again entered as a works driver with Giancarlo Baghetti in the Sarthe marathon. Baghetti was, unfortunately, involved in an accident near Maison Blanche in Peter Bolton's AC Cobra, an episode that cost the lives of three spectators who had stopped in an area prohibited to the public. Above: the 275 P driven by Frenchman Jean Guichet and Nino Vaccarella won the race, preceding a private 250 LM. For the French it was a return to success at Le Mans after 10 years, while for the Italian drivers the "famine" would start from the following year and come to an end 20 years later.

1965
First at Le Mans for the last time

The year 1965 was the first in the official challenge by Ford for the Ferrari crown in world sports car racing. The result was, substantially, a draw with the Americans winners of the International Grand Touring Constructors' Championship thanks to the Shelby Cobra Daytona, the cars that had preceded the famous Ford GT40, the car that competed against the various two seater Ferraris in 1965, among them the 250 LM, the 275 P2 and the 330 P2 for the dominance in the International Prototype Trophy.

The start was a Sebring without the works Ferraris, won by the futuristic Chaparral with a 250 LM driven by David Piper and Tony Maggs third behind the Miles-McLaren Ford. At Monza's first world championship 1,000 Kilometres, victory went to the 275 P2 of Mike Parkes and Jean Guichet with Ford third. Driving the same car, Nino Vaccarella and Lorenzo Bandini triumphed at the Targa Florio for which Ford sent a single GT40 that retired. The next race at the Nürburgring went in the Italians' favour with the 300 P2 of John Surtees and Ludovico Scarfiotti the winner. Then for the most important race of them all, Le Mans, and the two constructors prepared themselves in the best way possible with an overall total of 22 cars among their GTs and prototypes. Despite all the works cars from the Prancing Horse having to retire – the same thing happened to Ford – the win still went to Ferrari with a 250 LM entered by Maranello's American importer Luigi Chinetti and driven by Jochen Rindt and Masten Gregory to score the victory that remains even today as Ferrari's last win in the French endurance classic.

Among the GTs, the privately entered Ferrari 275 GTB/C driven by Willy Mairesse and "Beurlys" came third and first in class. But the next rounds in the championship would not be enough for Ferrari to overtake the Shelby in the GT

category. With 1966 on the horizon, new regulations were introduced and the challenge between the two constructors would continue, especially at Le Mans where the Americans triumphed by fielding a number of cars and resources that their Italian rivals could not match.

The 1,000 Kilometres of Monza was run on 25 April. Between the works and private cars, Ferrari took six places in the first seven on the grid. The win went to Mike Parkes and Jean Guichet in a 275 P2. Top: the Frenchman following Lorenzo Bandini's 330 P2 but would not be able to pass the wheel to his crew mate Nino Vaccarella because he had to retire on the ninth of 100 laps due to a suspension breakage. Above: the Ferrari 330 P2 photographed from the same position on the Parabolica corner with John Surtees, who would alternate with Ludovico Scarfiotti, at the wheel and would come second. At Monza, Maranello entered a new works Dino 166 P for Baghetti-Biscaldi but it retired on the second lap.

Above: Ludovico Scarfiotti at the start of the Trento-Bondone, a round in the European Mountain Climb Championship. The Italian is driving a victorious Dino 166 P, which Maranello entered both for the Continental hillclimb and for a number of counters in the world sports racing car championship, taking fourth place in the 1,000 Kilometres of the Nürburgring driven by Bandini-Vaccarella. The car's meagre cubic capacity, which was little more than 1500, was obtained by modifying the victorious 6-cylinder engine of the 156, winner of the Formula 1 World Championship of four years earlier.Below, left: Nino Vaccarella's 275 P2 at the Targa Florio. Two weeks after the triumph at Monza, Vaccarella won the Sicilian classic with Bandini, the first of his three home wins. In '65 the win was all Italian, with an incredible Vaccarella and Lorenzo Bandini, who drove the Ferrari V12 in the central part of the race.

Below, right: refuelling and re-tyring the winning 250 LM at Le Mans. Next to the car is American Masten Gregory, crew mate of Austrian Jochen Rindt sitting in the driver's seat. In front of the bespectacled driver from Kansas is the snowy head of "Sparky" Tramonti, the long-time Ferrari mechanic who mainly worked in Formula 1. After he joined the works team, his drivers scored many successes in the mid-Seventies, among them Niki Lauda and Clay Regazzoni.

The top rivals of the best years

In the beginning, Enzo Ferrari and Ferrari itself have always found in motor racing the main reason for being. That was understood in 1963 when Ford were within an ace of acquiring his small but famous company. The patriarch of Maranello kept the motor sport part as a priority and that says a lot about his interest in that world. But the failure of the negotiations was a kind of detonator of the rivalry with the American industrial giant that led to a bitter battle on the track. In part, Ferrari was subjected to the same situation as of a few years earlier with the slight of Tony Vandervell, who founded Vanwall to beat Ferrari and he did it a number of times. The modern Goliath was Ford, which had resources that Italians could only dream of and in the end logic led the American giant to beat the little David (at Le

Mans in 1966). Revenge came in the form of the victorious parade of Ferraris across the Daytona finish line in 1967; a spectacle that would remain the most famous even if not the highest point in the legendary war of the Sixties, with only one point in favour of Ferrari.

If Ford was big, the same could be said of Porsche, which in the meantime prepared to challenge the two warriors. In Germany, a series of extraordinary two seaters were built that had their culmination with the 917. It was in 1969 and Ferrari tried uselessly for three years to beat the lethal weapon from Stuttgart which, with the irony of chance, carried a prancing horse as its symbol. But it was the federal regulations that brought an end to that unbeatable monster, while at Ferrari they put the finishing tou-

Opposite: two Ford GT40s and two Porsche 908s throw themselves at the terrible big corner at Monza. It is the start of the 1968 1,000 Kilometres, a season officially deserted by Ferrari. Below: the Alfa Romeo 33TT3 being driven by Andrea De Adamich. The race is the 1,000 Kilometres of Brands Hatch, which the Italian won with Frenchman Henri Pescarolo. Alfa won three times that year, but the company would have to wait until 1975 to win the World Sports Car Championship. In the two previous years the title went to Matra, which leads the field (top right) in the 1973 1,000 Kilometres of the Nürburgring, Ferrari's last overall win. Behind the Matra MS670 of François Cevert is the winning Jackie Ickx-Brian Redman Ferrari 312 PB. Above, left: the Porsche 917 K of Helmut Marko and Gijs van Lennep, who won Le Mans in 1971. The German 12-cylinder was the most successful in that period of great splendour in the WSCC, which outclassed Formula 1 in terms of prestige and spectators at the circuits.

ches to the 312 P adopting, among other things, a flat 12-cylinder engine that won and convinced in Formula 1. In the meantime, a Ferrari rival went back to the track that the Scuderia always watched with careful attention: Alfa Romeo. The group, headed by an ex-Ferrarista, the irascible Tuscan Carlo Chiti, every now and then appeared, but it would have to await the departure of Maranello to win the title. The British with Lola and Mirage were not really challengers of any substance, as was the case years earlier with the spectacular Chaparral from the United States; a car that disappointed rather than convinced. From the confines of France – while waiting for Renault's programmes to reach completion – came the Matra programme with even more warlike intentions. The company's directors,

now disillusioned with Formula 1, anticipated Ferrari by a year and chose between sports car racing and Formula 1. The decision was for the two seaters and 1973 became the best season for this kind of racing. The battle was a winner, until the French scored three victories on the trot, including the 6 Hours of Watkins Glen. This was the last race of the season for Ferrari and, even if nobody knew at the time, it was also the end of Maranello's story in sports car racing, at least in official form. Other Ferraris challenged their rivals in later years at Le Mans, Monza, Daytona and Spa; all circuits were prestigious stages of endurance racing for decades. They also won, but the taste was not the same as when the articulated lorries used to leave Maranello passing under the boss's office window.

1967
That day at Daytona

At the end of 1966, Ferrari introduced the weapon with which it would try to claw back the prototype title. It was the 330 P4, which had a more imposing shape than the P3 as well as an increase of around 30 hp. Its debut was one of the most fortunate, winning the 24 Hours of Daytona driven by Lorenzo Bandini and newly acquired New Zealander Chris Amon.

To make the moment a historic one, motor sport director Franco Lini made the second placed P4 of Mike Parkes and Ludovico Scarfiotti and a P3 driven by Pedro Rodriguez and Jean Guichet cross the finish line three abreast. The picture of that show of strength was beamed around the world and gave even more emphasis to the happening; a few months later, the new 365 GTB4 two seater sports saloon would be dubbed the Daytona. Maranello did not compete in the 12 Hours of Sebring but it did in Europe at the end of April in the 1,000 Kilometres of Monza where Ferrari all but repeated the American result with the P4 taking the first two places. There was just enough time to load the only car entered for the 1,000 Kilometres of Spa-Francorchamps

Left: a rear view of the new 330 P4. The car took over from the P2 and P3 and had a revised aerodynamic design, but it was preferred to work on the existing mechanics and power unit to achieve better performance. The engine cover hides a 60° V12 of 4-litres that put out 450 hp.
Right: two of the 11 works drivers fielded by Ferrari in that lucky season.

Mike Parkes (left) talks to new acquisition Chris Amon. The British engineer ended his career as a sports car racer with second place in the 1967 Le Mans and continued with the consent of Enzo Ferrari to race for private teams. Amon began the season in the best way with two victories in his first two races at Daytona and Monza.

of 1 May, where Parkes and Scarfiotti came fifth, before the team moved off to Monaco for the imminent Grand Prix. Sadly, the Lorenzo Bandini tragedy was played out on the streets of Monte Carlo; a death that shook Ferrari to its foundations once more.

The subsequent Targa Florio and 1,000 Kilometres of the Nürburgring were two triumphs by Porsche. The Stuttgart team then presented itself as the most credible rival for the world title. Ford, which had practically deserted the championship but still had the sole objective of repeating the 1966 Le Mans victory, prepared for the French race with even more cars compared to the previous one and entered no

Left: the Bandini-Amon 330 P4 (foreground) in the paddock of the 1,000 Kilometres of Monza. Next to it (12) is the works Dino 206 S crewed by Jonathan Williams and Gunther Klass.
The barchetta, a past winner of the European Mountainclimb Championship, did not distinguish itself at Monza and had to retire in the early stages of the race due to cylinder head problems. Right: a close-up of the unforgettable Lorenzo Bandini. In his sixth season as a works Ferrari driver, the Milanese was ready to reap the advantage of a great deal of work. Victories in the two opening races of the World Sports Car Championship had galvanised him. In Formula 1, he was forced by team choice to miss the first race in South Africa but looked forward to the imminent Grand Prix of Monaco as a fundamental opportunity to climb the world championship table. Unfortunately, the Monegasque race proved to be fatal and Italian motor racing had to wait many years before boasting a driver able to return to the top of F1. Below: the Ferrari 412 P assigned to Pedro Rodriguez and Jean Guichet. The car was really a 330 P3 with updated mechanics and run, as Enzo Ferrari wished, by private teams. On the aesthetic front, however, there were no great changes to the P3 and P4. Among the privateers was the North American Racing Team of the Commendatore's friend Luigi Chinetti, who had always been extremely close to Maranello.

fewer than seven prototypes. Ferrari responded with eight works and private cars, fully aware of the fact that Ford would do anything to cancel out the dramatic defeat at Daytona. After a day's racing, four laps separated the Parkes-Scarfiotti P4 from the Mark IV of winners Dan Gurney and A.J. Foyt. That result satisfied Ford which, soon afterwards, announced its retirement from racing, while Ferrari was left to complete its last race before winning the world title, the 6 Hours of

Brands Hatch. Porsche was the only other constructor with the chance of overtaking Maranello for the championship. Ferrari went to the British circuit with three P4s and a new team of drivers, among whom was the young Scottish star of motor racing, Jackie Stewart. It was the future triple F1 champion and crewman Chris Amon who scored the points that enabled the Scuderia to win the constructors' over 2,000 cc title, while the World Sports Car Championship went to Ford after the victories of the various GT40s in the face of the useless opposition of a number of private 250 LMs. Ford's abandonment, together with the new 1968 regulations, induced Enzo Ferrari to keep out of sports car racing officially the following year. In addition, the financial situation of Maranello was ever more delicate, with Fiat just around the corner ready to become Ferrari's majority shareholder in June 1969; an agreement that enabled the Prancing Horse to enter works cars in five different categories, including hillclimbs and America's Can-Am.

A cutaway of the 330 P4, the car that brought the WSCC back to Maranello after it had slipped through their fingers and into the hands of the mighty Ford the previous year. Among the details that distinguish the two Ferraris can be seen new rims, aluminium reinforcement of the chassis and a new cylinder head that took the number of valves from two to three for each cylinder.

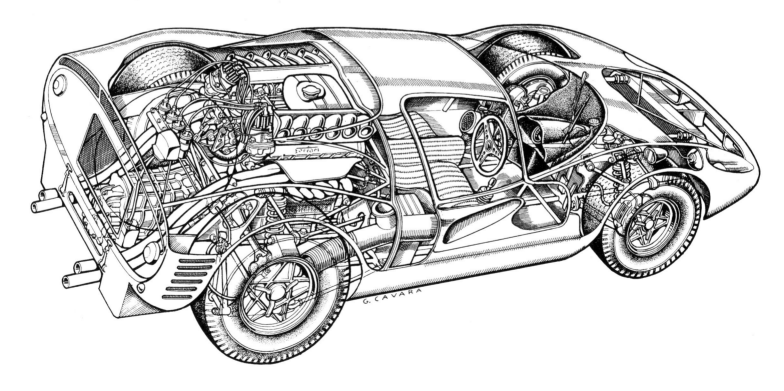

Monza, Italy, the test bed par excellence on which Enzo Ferrari often depended to confirm or relaunch the image of his racing cars. For fixture reasons, the 1,000 Kilometres was one of the opening rounds of the sports racing season, while the Grand Prix was always held, as it is today, in September and usually closed the European season. Enzo Ferrari often attended practice days, attempting to provide the support that only the Boss knows how to give. When he was not in the pits, he left everything to his track squad that included Mauro Forghieri, who was certainly the most important intermediary. Above, right: the Modenese engineer is shown while waiting for Ludovico Scarfiotti's 330 P4 to go out, taking time to exchange impressions, and then it was time for the mechanics to go to work.

Above, left: the sister car of Lorenzo Bandini and Chris Amon during another pause in Monza practice. The driver getting into the car here is Bandini, winner of his home race.

Below: the private Dino 206 S of Mario Casoni and "Shangry-la" having retired with engine trouble, while at the top of the southern banking is the Pedro Rodriguez-Jean Guichet 412 P, which retired mid-race following an accident.

1972
Absolute domination

The 312 P made its official debut on 10 January 1971 at the 1,000 Kilometres of Buenos Aires in the hands of Ignazio Giunti (top) and Arturo Merzario. Sadly, soon after the halfway mark an incredible accident cost the driver from Rome his life, he having changed with Merzario a few laps earlier. The rest of the season would see Jacky Ickx at the wheel of the 312 P, who would be entered alternatively with Clay Regazzoni and Mario Andretti. Above: the extremely wet start of the 1,000 Kilometres of Monza on 25 April, with the Ickx and Peterson Ferraris on the front row. Behind them juts the nose of the third 312 P in the event; Maranello knew no adversaries that day.

After its return to sports car racing with the 312 P in 1969, a car however which left no special memories in the history of Ferrari, for the next year Maranello developed and built the 512 S, a two seater powered by a 5-litre engine of classic 60° V12 configuration. This sensational car did not achieve the hoped for results and is only remembered for its extraordinary victory at the 12 Hours of Sebring with Ignazio Giunti and Nino Vaccarella, who were joined during the last stages of the race by Italo-American Mario Andretti. In the meantime, Ford left the scene so Porsche began to monopolise sports car racing, first with the 908 and, from the last victorious debut race of 1969 – the Grand Prix of Austria – with the formidable 917.

For 1971 Ferrari modified the 512 and replaced the S in its designation with an M and entrusted the new car to private teams that had been working with Maranello for some time. A new version of the 312 P was built for the works team called the PB, with the second letter to indicate the new 12-cylinder boxer engine to distinguish it from the model of two years earlier. Unfortunately, the first example was destroyed in a dramatic accident that cost Giunti his life during the 1,000 Kilometres of Buenos Aires. Subsequent races brought just a few points results. The only victory was in the 9 Hours of Kyalami with Clay Regazzoni and Brian Redman at the end of the year, which was not a world championship counter.

For 1972 Ferrari intended to do things in a big way and succeeded, all eased by new regulations that excluded the potent 5-litres, including the dominant Porsche 917. The only challenger was Alfa Romeo, which gave Enzo Ferrari a special charge and from that direct face-to-face came out

Top, left: the start at the Targa Florio of the 312 P, driven by Arturo Merzario and Sandro Munari, the latter already a famous rally driver, having recently won the Monte Carlo in a Lancia Fulvia HF. Recruited unexpectedly by Enzo Ferrari, he and Merzario won on the roads of Sicily and after that were entered for the 1,000 Kilometres of Zeltweg in which they came fourth. After time spent at Abarth, in 1970 Arturo joined Ferrari. For the first two seasons he was the Maranello test driver, occasionally competing in WSCC races, but with little to show for it. Later, he contributed to Ferrari's victories before moving on to Alfa Romeo when the Scuderia retired from endurance racing.

Top, right: three of the 10 works drivers taken on during the year by Enzo Ferrari. From left to right they are Mario Andretti, winner of four WSCC rounds in 1972, Clay Regazzoni, who only won at Monza with Jacky Ickx and Ickx himself (right), who won at Brands Hatch and Zeltweg as well as the trio of North American races at Daytona, Sebring and Watkins Glen.

Below: Jacky Ickx during a pit stop on his way to winning the 1,000 Kilometres of Monza, where the mechanics' contribution was, as always, fundamental. But while their work ended with the start of the race in Grands Prix, in endurance racing the contribution of these men was absolutely central to the result, both during routine work and in cases of emergency.

of it severely beaten, with Maranello winning all the 10 races in which it competed.

The only race Ferrari did not enter was the 24 Hours of Le Mans, despite having set the first and third fastest times in Sarthe testing in March with Jacky Ickx and Clay Regazzoni, saying that trouble with the clutch found at the time would be difficult to resolve for such a long and technically stressful race. To take on the season, the team availed itself of the services of drivers involved in a stable plan in the world championship, Ickx and Regazzoni, , adding another eight including world famous rallyist Sandro Munari, who won the Targa Florio together with Arturo

Merzario. Ferrari achieved the maximum at the Austrian 1,000 Kilometres, its cars taking the top four places; a supremacy that explains itself due to the few adversaries which, excluding the Alfa Romeo 33TT3s on some occasions, made the rounds of this world championship like a simple monologue for Maranello. Among the Grand Tourers, the famous Daytona achieved a number of class successes, which did not permit Ferrari to counter the all-powerful Porsche 911.

For 1973, competition strengthened in prototype racing. Matra took the title from Ferrari at the last race, the Scuderia having won at Monza and the Nürburgring, the last two sports car races in its history.

During the winter of that year, Ferrari carried out some tests with a new version of the 312 PB but the decision was taken at the last minute not to challenge Matra, Alfa Romeo, Porsche and Mirage, preferring to devote all its efforts to a rebirth in Formula 1. In just a few months, the results proved the company right.

The Peterson-Schenken 312 P decelerating for the Parabolica during the 1,000 Kilometres of Monza. The two seater was powered by a flat 12-cylinder unit that was also used for two seasons in the 312 B F1, the 1972 version of which developed about 450 hp. At the end of its career in 1980,

the car's power output had abundantly exceeded 500 hp. As well as in conquering the 1972 World Sports Car Championship, the engine proved fundamental in the years that followed for Ferrari's return to the top of Formula 1, when it was used to power the glorious T series.

Top, left: a close-up of Ronnie Peterson, runner-up in the previous year's F1 World Championship, who was a WSCC regular in 1972, contributing excellent results to Ferrari's world title chase.

Top, centre: Peterson brings his 312 P into the Brands Hatch pits during practice for the 1,000 Kilometres. The picture is a testimony to the logistics situation in which world level races were organised.

Top, right: Mario Andretti as he tried to pass a Chevrolet Nova in his victorious 12 Hours of Sebring, the first of the three counters held in the United States, all won by the Italo-American with Jacky Ickx.

Centre page: Clay Regazzoni in the 6 Hours of Daytona in which he came fourth with Brian Redman.

Below: a Ferrari at Daytona between an Alfa Romeo 33TT3 and a Lola T280, the only two cars which, although with no results, attempted to "worry" the unbeatable 312 P. Matra could also have competed against Ferrari, but it preferred not to enter the other races and concentrated its efforts on the 24 Hours of Le Mans, a race in which Maranello did not compete.

Palmarès
Formula 1

1952	World Championship for Drivers (Alberto ASCARI)
1953	World Championship for Drivers (Alberto ASCARI)
1956	World Championship for Drivers (Juan Manuel FANGIO)
1958	World Championship for Drivers (Mike HAWTHORN)
1961	World Championship for Drivers (Phil HILL)
1961	Constructors' Cup
1964	World Championship for Drivers (John SURTEES)
1964	Constructors' Cup
1975	World Championship for Drivers (Niki LAUDA)
1975	Constructors' Cup
1976	Constructors' Cup
1977	World Championship for Drivers (Niki LAUDA)
1977	Constructors' Cup
1979	World Championship for Drivers (Jody SCHECKTER)
1979	Constructors' Cup
1982	World Championship for Constructors
1983	World Championship for Constructors
1999	World Championship for Constructors
2000	World Championship for Drivers (Michael SCHUMACHER)
2000	World Championship for Constructors
2001	World Championship for Drivers (Michael SCHUMACHER)
2001	World Championship for Constructors
2002	World Championship for Drivers (Michael SCHUMACHER)
2002	World Championship for Constructors
2003	World Championship for Drivers (Michael SCHUMACHER)
2003	World Championship for Constructors
2004	World Championship for Drivers (Michael SCHUMACHER)
2004	World Championship for Constructors
2007	World Championship for Drivers (Kimi RAIKKONEN)
2007	World Championship for Constructors
2008	World Championship for Constructors

❏ From 1950 to 2008, 803 world level races took place in 27 countries for a total of 36 different championships. Ferrari has competed in all of these Grands Prix with the exception of 10 500 Miles of Indianapolis, which were world championship counters until 1960, and 15 Grands Prix. The last time Ferrari did not compete in a race officially, practice included, was in 1976 in Austria. The last time Ferrari did not start in a Grand Prix was six years later in the Grand Prix of Switzerland at Dijon.

❏ Until 1957, Ferraris entered by other teams or private individuals competed in races. The largest number did so in 1952, when 25 non-works cars took to the track, with a second place being scored by Swiss Rudi Fischer in his home race. In 1961, Giancarlo Baghetti ran in three races in a single seater managed by Maranello but entered by a different team. After that, between 1964 and 1969, there were a number of works entries, including decisive final races, which gave the title to John Surtees and in which the Italian team competed through its United States importer NART.

❏ The Grand Prix of Germany is the GP in which Ferrari scored more victories than any other, 19 wins out of 54 races. There then follow the GPs of France and Italy with 17 victories each, two more than those in Britain and Belgium. Ferrari did not win either of the two world championship Grands Prix of Las Vegas, Pacific or Luxembourg in which it competed and also did not do so the only time it entered the GPs of Pescara, Morocco, Dallas or Singapore. And it achieved no victories in the 11 500 Miles of Indianapolis as it declined to compete, except in 1952.

❏ The number of different models built by Ferrari for Formula 1 total 56, almost one per year, 42 of which won at least one race and that have made history, like the F2002 and F2004; each of them scored 15 victories. The legendary 500 F2 also had a fine success rate in 1952-3, winning 14 Grands Prix. Of the cars' engines, the flat 12 – dubbed the boxer – should be remembered as it competed in 11 seasons between 1970 and 1980, won 37 GPs and 7 drivers' and constructors' world championships.

❏ The 72 Ferrari works F1 drivers came from 17 different countries. There were 24 Italians, followed by 10 British and the same number of French. Half of them were able to win Grands Prix with the record, which is unlikely to be equalled, belonging to Michael Schumacher with 74 victories in 11 seasons and 186 races. Others who left their mark before the German ace were Alberto Ascari with 13 wins, which was exceeded 20 years later by Niki Lauda with his 15.

❏ As well as the 9 Ferrari men who won world drivers' championships, there are others who, with their results, contributed to Maranello winning the 16 F1 world constructors' titles and Trophies instituted from 1958. The points scored by Richie Ginther, Giancarlo Baghetti and Wolfgang von Trips added to those of Phil Hill gave Ferrari its first title in 1961. Three years later, John Surtees and Lorenzo Bandini won the second, while it is necessary to wait until the 70s to see Ferrari at the top of the list again. 3 times with Lauda, 2 with Clay Regazzoni and one with Carlos Reutemann, the drivers contributed to an equal number of titles. In 1982-3 the results of Gilles Villeneuve, Didier Pironi, Mario Andretti, Patrick Tambay and René Arnoux contributed to writing Ferrari's name on the role of honour twice. Then there was another wait 16 years long before Eddie Irvine supported by Mika Salo of Finland, who took the place of the injured Schumacher for six races, brought a title back to Maranello before the Michael Schumacher-Rubens Barrichello duo enabled Ferrari to monopolise the championships for five consecutive years. In the last two years, the Prancing Horse has won an equal number of titles due to the results achieved by Kimi Raikkonen and Felipe Massa. In fact, if the constructors' championship had existed at the beginning of Formula 1, Ferrari would certainly have won it in 1952, 1953 and 1956.

Palmarès
Sports, Grand Touring, Prototypes, Constructors

1953	World Sports Car Championship
1954	World Sports Car Championship
1956	World Sports Car Championship
1957	World Sports Car Championship
1958	World Sports Car Championship
1960	World Sports Car Championship
1961	World Sports Car Championship
1962	Over 2000 cc International Grand Touring Championship for Constructors
1962	Over 3000 cc Sports Car Cup
1963	Over 2000 cc International Grand Touring Championship for Constructors
1963	International Prototypes Trophy
1964	Over 2000 cc International Grand Touring Championship for Constructors
1965	International Prototypes Trophy
1967	Over 2000 cc International Prototypes Trophy for Constructors
1972	International Manufacturers' Championship

❏ From 1953 to 1973, 147 world championship sports car races were organised and staged on 19 circuits in nine different countries. Works Ferraris competed in all seasons, except 1968, for a total of 114 events.

❏ During the same period, Ferraris entered by other teams or private individuals competed in such races. At least one non-works Ferrari raced in 129 events. There were only seven races for which neither works nor private Ferraris were entered, and they were the 1953 and 1958 Tourist Trophy, 1968 1000 Kilometres of Spa, the 1968 and 1969 1000 Kilometres of Zeltweg, the 1969 Targa Florio and the 6 Hours of Watkins Glen.

❏ The Italian constructor won on at least 15 of the 19 circuits that hosted world championship endurance races. Works Ferraris did not win the 500 Kilometres of Bridgehampton, the 6 Hours of Vallelunga or the 1000 Kilometres of Dijon. They won 56 races, a success rate of 40%, and were victorious in nine 12 Hours of Sebring, one more that in the 24 Hours of Le Mans, which has always been the most prestigious endurance event.

❏ The most successful two seater was the 312 P of 1972 with 10 wins out of 10 races. There were another two victories the following year, which made the car the most successful sports racer. But other models built at Maranello also went down in endurance racing history, like the 250 Testa Rossa which, in its various evolutions, totalled 11 wins between 1958 and 1962.

❏ Eighty-three drivers competed in the works sports car team with 20 of them, among whom the future triple F1 world champion Jackie Stewart, were entered by Maranello at least once. There were eight seasons of works competition from 1955 to 1962 for Phil Hill and Olivier Gendebien. But the award for most races has to go to Jacky Ickx with 33 appearances between 1970 and 1973, four more than Phil Hill who, however, won the most, 12 victories against the 10 of Gendebien and Ickx's eight. Among the Italians, the one who competed in most races was Ludovico Scarfiotti who, between 1959 and 1967, raced sports cars for eight seasons and a total of 30 races.

❏ In total, Ferrari won 56 times, seven of which with cars entered by private teams. The drivers who were able to win in a Maranello built car number 44, 17 of whom repeated their success in F1.

❏ Thirteen nations provided Ferrari with winning drivers, with Italy at the top of the list on 14. There then follow the British with six winners, one more than the Belgians, and Americans.

❏ Forty-two different teams won the 56 sports car races with Ferraris over 20 years. Individual winners include Giannino Marzotto, Eugenio Castellotti and Piero Taruffi in the last of the Mille Miglias and Umberto Maglioli in the 1954 Carrera Panamericana to the Americans Dan Gurney, Chuck Daigh and Phil Hill who, together with Belgian Olivier Gendebien, alternated in the Testa Rossa winning at Sebring in 1959. The most successful pair of drivers was P. Hill and Gendebien with six wins, including three in the 24 Hours of Le Mans. After them come the Mario Andretti and Jacky Ickx duo with four victories in the unforgettable 1972 season.

❏ There are top drivers among those who raced for private teams who, in the parallel Formula 1, often raced to beat Ferrari. The top names included Stirling Moss, future world champions Graham Hill, Denny Hulme, Jochen Rindt, Jackie Stewart and Mario Andretti. Winner Phil Hill also raced in many other world championship events with private teams before joining the works squad. The same thing went for Mexican Pedro Rodriguez who, unfortunately, died in a two seater Ferrari in a non-championship race in 1971.

❏ Among the private teams that fielded Ferraris, sometimes with the direct technical and logistical support of the factory, were especially NART of the United States, Britain's Maranello Concessionaires, Belgians Ecurie Francorchamps and Equipe Nationale Belge, while the Italian team Scuderia Centro-Sud won the sole 4 Hours of Pescara in 1961.

Giorgio Nada Editore Srl

Editorial manager
Leonardo Acerbi

Editorial coordination
Diana Calarco

Graphic design and cover
Furuya Yoshihito

Translation
Robert Newman

Fotographs:
Automobile Club Milano
Enrico Mapelli
Giorgio Nada Editore
Giorgio Proserpio
ELLE EMME
Actualfoto
Danilo Recalcati
Erminio Ferranti

Acknowledgments:
Pino Allievi
Gianni Cancellieri
Gianni Cattaneo

Giorgio Nada Editore
Via Claudio Treves, 15/17
I – 20090 VIMODRONE MI
Tel. +39 02 27301126
Fax +39 02 27301454
E-mail: info@giorgionadaeditore.it
http://www.giorgionadaeditore.it

**The catalogue of Giorgio Nada Editore publications
is available on request at the above address.**

Distributed by:
Giunti Editore Spa
via Bolognese 165
I – 50139 FIRENZE
www.giunti.it

Ferrari's World Champions
ISBN: 978-88-7911-467-7

Printed by
Giunti Industrie Grafiche (Prato),
october 2009